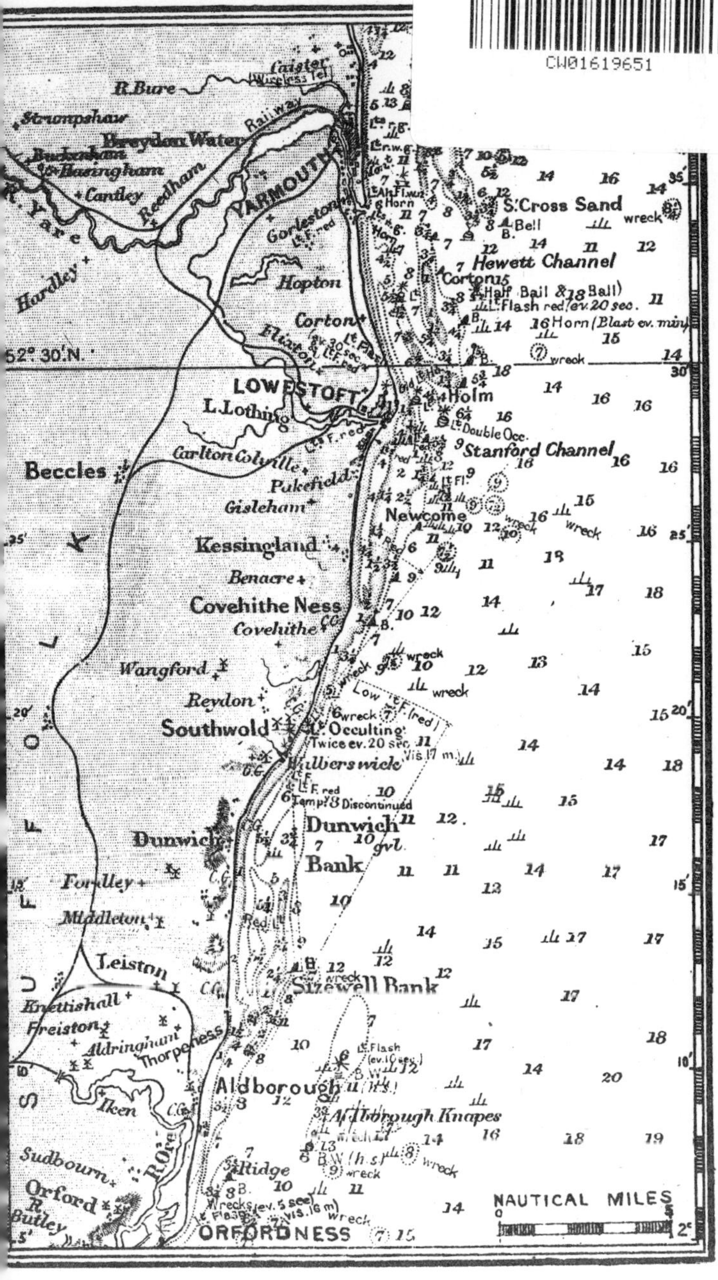
Caister
Wireless Tel.
R.Bure
Strumpshaw
Breydon Water
Railway
Buckenham
& Hasingham
Cantley
Reedham
R. Yare
YARMOUTH
Gorleston
Hardley
Hopton
Corton
S.t Cross Sand
Bell
wreck
Hewett Channel
Half Bail & Ball)
Flash red (ev. 20 sec.
Horn (Blast ev. min)
52° 30′N.
LOWESTOFT
L. Lothing
Holm
Double Occ.
Stanford Channel
Carlton Colville
Beccles
Pakefield
Gisleham
Newcome
Kessingland
Benacre
Covehithe Ness
Covehithe
Wangford
Reydon
Southwold
Occulting
Twice ev. 20 sec.
Vis 17 m.
Walberswick
Discontinued
Dunwich
Dunwich
Bank
Fordley
Middleton
Red Lt
Leiston
Sizewell Bank
Knettishall
Freiston
Aldringham
Thorpeness
Flash
Aldborough
Aldborough Knapes
Iken
R. Ore
Sudbourn
Ridge
Orford
R. Butley
Wrecks
ORFORDNESS
NAUTICAL MILES
SUFFOLK

SUFFOLK SEA-BORDERS

By the same Author

SHOALWATER AND FAIRWAY

Conway Maritime Press

THE LOW CLIFF-LINE AT SOUTHWOLD

SUFFOLK SEA-BORDERS

by

H. Alker Tripp
('Leigh Hoe')

Illustrated by the Author

CONWAY MARITIME PRESS
1972

ISBN 085177 058 4

First published in 1926

Printed in Great Britain by Latimer Trend & Co. Ltd.,
Whitstable, Kent

NOTE

EARLIER wayfarers of the Suffolk coast, who have written of its open landscape and its history, have come to it by way of the tracks along-shore. Following with a kindred eye, the present writer has reached it from the sea. The same cliffs, shingle-banks and havens are here; the angle of vision alone is changed.

CONTENTS

LIST OF ILLUSTRATIONS

IN MONOCHROME

IN LINE

LIST OF ILLUSTRATIONS

CHAPTER I

OUT OF LONDON RIVER

LONDON RIVER only comes into the picture by way of contrast.

Her jib aback, the yacht had turned on her heel, clearing a crowded company of barges at anchor. Down the Lower Hope (below Gravesend) she drove seaward — her bowsprit pointed for the moment at the wharves, masts, funnels and oil-reservoirs of Thames Haven. Once past the Mucking and Lower Hope Point, she would open the grey distance of Sea Reach, and would be headed for the North Sea.

"Grey" is the inevitable word, for, even on the finest day, a certain greyness is felt through all the colour scheme. Smoke drifts, and the broken water is turbid; even in full sunlight that greyness is there. Just as Whistler sometimes employed black pigment as a harmoniser, a subtle quality running uniformly throughout his colour, so Thames-side tinges her atmosphere with sympathetic grey. And as Whistler, with his shadowy sense of black, obtained a subtlety of tone and depth, so also does Thames-side. In both cases the key of the symphony is lowered, but the "quality" (using the word as the painter understands it) is infallibly enhanced.

We were away. It was three in the afternoon, and a strong south-westerly wind was breaking the waves into foam. It had whistled in our rigging when we lay at anchor, but now—running free—we were losing all sound of wind. Only the blown water and bellying white curves of sail betrayed it.

"Funny thing," Robinson had said, when he first came on board yesterday, "I've never set foot on a yacht before in my life." And this, as I had warned him, was no brass-bound packet. Built on smack lines, *Irene* had no smallest touch of gilt in her whole composition. Robinson, slim and exquisite, had looked a trifle out of his element at first sight; but he appraised her merits with a comprehending eye. He found much to approve.

"Seems to me you've got most things in this

little concern," he said, after finishing his inspection. We were at anchor then. From compass, clock and barometer to stoves and grocery-locker, his scrutiny had wandered everywhere, with a running chatter of question and comment. I do not want to flatter the youngster (" youngster " I call him, for he is still in the twenties), but his clear-cut face is a pleasant thing to look at; and he has a smile that drifts over it and fades like sunshine across a landscape. The simile is over-poetical, but no other can adequately render the fact. And, with all his grace, he is tough as whipcord, and all man.

" Yes," he had added, with easy patronage, as we emerged from the cabin and went on deck, " the little box is full of tricks. All found. Put the old thing on wheels, and you've got a nice little caravan."

That was two days ago; in space of two days his outlook had been oddly varied.

I had put him on at the helm almost at once, and his natural aptitude leaped to the eye. He never made the same mistake twice, and, with a cricketer's eye and hand, he was swift and decisive. But he ran the full gamut of error, without which no man can learn; he made his mistakes, and the old yacht, while he sailed her, was like some well-bred and experienced horse under the touch of a novice. She suffered him, but not without reproof. Sitting beside a clumsy driver, I have watched the protest and surprise in every line of the horse's body. So, in every curve of her, can a yacht cry shame upon a futile helmsman. And Robinson—sensitive always—felt it; she was no longer to him a box afloat—she was alive. And he hungered to find himself approved.

"She *upbraids* me every time," he told me with a laugh, half amused and half regretful; "I can't help feeling she'd do it better if I left her alone." And he was not the first to have that same feeling about an old boat. I told him of one old smack which used to live at West Mersea in Essex.

In and out of that little channel to Mersea she had sailed for years. Finally she changed hands, being bought by some person fatuously inadequate, who on his first day—after mishandling her in every conceivable fashion—lost his bearings in Mersea Quarters and was in danger of running aground. Dismayed, he howled for advice to some smacksmen. "Leave her alone," they shouted back, "leave the old girl alone, and *she'll find her own way in*, I reckon."

In just this fashion the personality of *Irene* had impressed itself upon Robinson. Turning to windward in a seaway, he was almost spellbound, even after he had relinquished the tiller in my favour. He leaned in the well, his chin on his hands, looking for'ard. He watched her quickness and confidence as she rose to the wave, her directness and resolution as she drove—if need be—clean through the crest of it, tearing its fringes into sheets of drifting spray. The driven spray dripped in rivers from his face and oilskin, but he remained as if fascinated. She was living, she was beautiful.

He watched the green water that thudded on board and ran sluicing in a torrent over the battened fore-hatch. She lifted again, and the water gurgled away, pouring back through the scuppers. The sea pounded and hammered her. His face wet with the salt spray, he was absorbed, spell-bound.

That was yesterday. To-day we were running free with the wind on the quarter, and I had given him the tiller, while I stood or squatted heedfully beside him. The yacht had romped down Sea Reach, alive with its moving population of tugs, hoppers and coasters, of liners and barges. Not by the wind only, but by bluff prows numberless and by thrashing propellers, this broad highway was beaten into foam.

"Southend. Southend Pier."

His far-away intonation was everything; it conveyed, beyond reach of words, his sense of contrast. Southend was there with its long pier; at the one end was the typical sea-front, with its trippers and loafers and giggling flirtations; there were niggers and picture-halls. And here at the other was open seaway—road to all the ports of all the world. Southend was remote from us here, remote unutterably.

The pier had fallen astern; the seaward horizon was level and single, its long line broken only by distant shipping. And blurs of steamer-smoke smudged the low sky above it.

The chart, which I had shown to my young shipmate on his first day, had been one more revelation to him. The open waters upon which we were now entering are no unimpeded seaway; they are choked and beset by sands. The shoal-system covers an area of 500 square miles, here at the mouth of the Thames, complicating and barring the sea; it is a treacherous province. Many of its sandbanks dry out completely at low water; and only the chart unriddles the mystery for the unlearned, for the chart reveals in plan those narrow fairways—kept open by scour of the tides—that thread between them. Along the fairways, marked by lightships and beacons and by buoys innumerable, the shipping of the world shapes its final course for London.

The Nore Light Vessel was now a dwindling hull astern of us, a fixed item in the shifting group of brown-sailed barges and busy tramps about the mouth of the Medway.

Almost dreamy-eyed at times, Robinson was again absorbed in the witchery of swift and gracious movement under sail. It was more compelling than music. The youngster had in him what Coventry Patmore calls

> " The fair sum of six thousand years'
> Traditions of civility."

That reality of culture was there, and his response was sure.

The foam creamed away on both sides of us as we swung off northward, and the wind-furrowed sea was grey and spacious. The Mouse Light Vessel was abeam, and the yacht was heaving and again heaving forward with the movement of a following sea. There was a desolation about the water north-westward, empty under sullen skies; but to southward and eastward the main channels were still

populated with the shipping of the Port of London. The Essex shore had fallen apart from us, and we were at sea.

And we felt the immense uplift of it all—this oneness with buoyancy of wave and wind. Yesterday, as we thrashed to windward, we could realise in our own small way the pride of some old-time clipper. We, in these steamship fairways, are still of the ancient habit. Remote as we are from those lords of sail, we are yet of their ancient family :

> " Their true descendant, as the veriest hind
> May yet be sprung of kings."

More than one modern ocean-freighter, with her towering freeboard, with her derricks and samson-posts, passed us—outward bound. Bluff masses, they are stolid enough, as they follow the tracks of the Blackwall frigates and the heeling China clippers of the greatest century of sail. They pass, naked hulled, and with smoke blown from them. Theirs are now the seaways. But once, with a fair wind and a quartering sea, the old clippers would race swaying, with snowy canvas piled on snowy canvas aloft, with skysails and royal staysails set. Those days are gone for ever.

And not nowadays is the kicking wheel forced over by supreme effort of several struggling men. The blunt-bowed freighter of to-day, which buffets her way by sheer force of machinery, need make no call upon their muscle: with steering gear controlled by telemotor from the bridge, the wheel turns that way or this at a touch.

The yacht raced away north-eastward; her own fairway was now the Swin Channel, while the Barrow Deep lay closely parallel. The two are separated by the shoal and shallows of the Barrow Sand, mile after mile.

The fleets of sail have vanished, and though we felt—as men born out of due time—that our real kinship was with the dead, we were no whit the less conscious of the magical quality in this modern traffic. Its own gaunt beauty is always present, and the everlasting pageant of it remains. By day and by night we had watched the shipping. Always with that same heavy wave of white rolled back from purposeful bows, always with that same air of directness and power, always with the foam churned and tumbling in wake of the heavy propellers, the steamships entered or left the Thames. Here was the typical tanker, outward bound in light ballast, here the Scandinavian timber-ship, with her deck-cargo of pit-props, and here was some ship in general cargo, immersed with precision to the load-line; three-islander, well-decker, shelter-decker, every type was present. There were liners and tramps, there were cable-ships, dredgers, tugs.

These, with the cargo-handling appliances which they carried, those steel derricks and samson-posts of theirs, are items in a world-embracing system. The system is one. By rail or road ashore in every continent, and trade-routes at sea, the world's vast service of distribution and supply is maintained; and in its entirety it is a single system. Steamship or railway—or the dock-equipment that transfers from one to the other—all are mechanical. The outward-bounders have just left a world of noisy derricks and grabs and capstans, of gate-machinery, travelling cranes, of lattice-towers and lifts and coal-tips. And on the other side of the world, perhaps, the ship will dock again in just such a scene, with the eternal clatter and bustle among the sheds and warehouses, day and night. But, indeed, if modern dock-

appliances be absent from her port of destination in some far corner of the globe, she will not be disconcerted. She will handle her own cargo—her own steel derricks will swing ashore every bale and case that the stevedores have cunningly stowed in those spacious holds of hers.

We had talked of it all, long into the night, while—anchored in the Lower Hope last evening—we watched the shapes in the darkness. Side-lights of green and red and the masthead lights were clear as stars, but the bulk of hull and the sense of smoke above it—these were things half lost and mysterious. The very size of the ships was difficult to gauge, and one noticed only the scale of note, ranging from the toot-toot of the tramp to the deep booming from the liner's fog-horn.

Similarly, the weight of sound from the engines, the volume of the thud-thud-thud from the propellers, the crisp rustle of the bow-wave—these voices came to us, each in its own scale, over the night. Then, as the blurred shape slid by, the yacht rolled and rolled again to the heavy swell from her. The dark water about us re-settled to its normal heave and fall, wash-wash-washing along the hull.

The fascination of them held us, and here to-day we were again following their tracks. Over the whole open seaway the waves whitened, but the steel hulls drove through them unperturbed; they smashed each wave to spindrift, and clouds of thin spray, like sheets of rain, swept from them as they passed.

Evening was now approaching: with no pleasant colour of "quiet evenfall." Merely a tinge of grey more sullen was about us. The Maplin Pile Lighthouse had faded astern, and close aboard of us was the Swin Middle Light Vessel.

"You've never seen these outer waters at night?" I asked my shipmate. "No? You ought to. On a clear night, as you can guess, it's a maze and glitter of changing pin-pricks all along the horizons. In the old days before steam, when the coal trade was carried in the old collier-brigs, there were practically no lights at all; but there's such uncommon profusion now, it's almost overdone."

"Can't always tell t'other from which?"

"That's it" (and my smile of deprecation answered his). "The times they occult and flash are shown on the chart; but when the yacht's bucking like a rodeo pony, and the spray sweeping like solid rain in a thunderstorm . . . it's not always too simple. But some are quite distinctive. Swin Middle, very powerful white; Maplin, red; Mouse, green, and so on." [1]

Although controlled by a separate authority (Trinity House), all these things are in effect part of the machinery of the seaport of London. Its great water-system of various channels comprises, like a railway, its settled and permanent ways, its signals and regular traffic, its transit of passengers and goods. Day and night it carries on. We had been talking round the subject, but the complexities of modern commerce soon began to range beyond our scope. In every direction the ramifications were endless.

Coldly green in the half-light, the waves surged up astern of us, foam-crested. We lifted with a heave to the swelling mass of each one of them, and settled with a little tumult of foam into the trough as it passed. I was anxious to get through the Swin Spitway before dark, the channel being narrow and unlighted, and we were holding course for the bell-buoy. The Spitway is in a direct line seaward of Clacton, four or five miles off-shore.

Then we sighted the buoy, and then we heard the bell. "*Clang, clan-clang, clang*"; here it was, the Swin Spitway bell-buoy, rocking and ringing

[1] The Mouse is now red, green being reserved exclusively for wreck.

TWILIGHT AT GRAVESEND.

ON LONDON RIVER

lustily in this vigorous seaway. Night was closing apace, but we should make no mistake now.

In another hour, darkness was almost undisputed; and, in shelter of the shoals, the sea was immediately quieter. Not only that, but the wind had lost its body; it was falling lighter every minute. Better than all, the clouds to westward rifted, and laid bare a brown dusk of late afterglow. It was a blessed access to serenity.

"I don't want to get kicked for rhapsodising," Robinson told me, "but . . ."

"But what?" I prompted, for the thing seemed to be evading him, and I wanted to hear it.

"It's so extraordinary—this change," he said. "We were sort of tumbling and battling in a dirty green sea an hour ago, with a racket of noise and all that smother of soap-lather all around us, and now . . . why, we're *gliding*. There's barely a blessed sound; and it's all gone dreamy and indistinct and magical. We seem poised in it. We're simply in space. Where's anything, anyway? It's all vague; it's all dark and brown and shadowy, almost unreal. A miracle, I call it."

As he said, the change had been sudden, with the combined effect of shelter and failing wind. But all my own prosaic solicitude had reference, at the moment, to the question whether the wind would flatten out altogether; no, it seemed holding, light but steady. We sailed on.

He appeared disinclined to talk, and I kept the tiller. But there was another idea with which I wanted to stir a quite distinct train of imagination,

One of Nelson's Seventy Fours

and I broke silence after—it may be—an hour of almost soundless sailing.

"There was another change about nightfall," I suggested, "beside the change of weather. We left the big shipways with their steamers and machinery and wireless and light vessels and all the rest of it; and *we've come right out of the world.* So many creeks and inlets of the east coast are entirely primitive. The clock's almost stood still in these backwaters for a few hundred years."

He seized the idea with eagerness. "I think that the very notion was looming somewhere on the sky-line with me, too," he said, "but I couldn't quite put a name to it. Never had much head," he ingenuously added, "and what ideas I've got are all clouded and vague in this extraordinary sort of monstrous silence."

I said nothing, but waited. He was "putting a name to it," better than he knew.

"Yes, you push closer to the past at night," he went on. "Things don't get between. With some old brute of a grey tanker planked in front of you, or an ugly devil of a ship with a crowd of derricks instead of rigging, you can't somehow fancy the old shapes and shadows. But *here*, in this darkness, I could fancy anything here—old Vanderdecken, or anything else you please."

The dull brownness of the western sky had faded to grey, and there was only starlight and drifting cloud. Dark water faded to invisible horizons and the flat land was lost in night.

"I don't know the old rigs like you do," Robinson went on, " but I can fancy some old galley with one sail, sort of chap out of the Bayeux tapestry, coming up astern of us just now. Things ashore have changed beyond recognition since then; but all this " (and the gesture was comprehensive) " is *their* sea as much as ours. Unaltered. I wonder if ships really have ghosts."

This was a sudden new inspiration of his.

" Like Vanderdecken's ? " I hazarded.

" Not quite. That yarn is hung round the neck of the blasphemous old shellback himself, not round his ship. No. Our own personalities " (his tone had a note of apology, and he spoke laboriously) " are so defined that we won't believe in death; we claim immortality. And what about the old sailing ships ? Do they *really* go to junk and driftwood, after all they've been ? "

He shifted his elbows on the coach-roof, and rested his chin in his hands. He was only a vague outline in the darkness.

" I know I'm talking rot," he resumed, with level seriousness, " but I feel it like this. All those successive generations of ships have sailed here in storm and sunshine, alive and vigorous, heeling from the wind and smashing through the water. Think of them. Things like the *Great Harry*, or the *Golden Hind*, or Nelson's three-deckers, or . . . all the rest of them. Does *nothing* remain ? "

It expressed his mood; it was the mood of the mystery of the night. And if Socrates in full daylight admitted that

> " All that we know is—nothing can be known,"

then certainly, in this reticent seascape under the stars, we had not the effrontery to give an answer. There could be no assured denial of anything.

" Here, my son," I said, " you go for'ard and see if the anchor cable's all free. I'm going to chuck the hook in here, in just half a jiff."

" What, ain't we goin' anywhere ? " he asked, with a vague but eloquent glance at obscurity in general. " Where in the world are we ? " he laughed.

" Just on the edge of the Mersea flats ; it's quite shallow here, though a fair distance off-shore."

. . . . . .

I had taken the risk of an uneasy berth. And the weather did its utmost. After a few hours' sleep I was out on deck again. The wind had come up once more with the tide, and was blowing hard from the south. Had I anticipated so much wind, I should have crept on last night, up to a snugger berth in the Colne. Here, the yacht wallowed and rolled, with the seas breaking all about her. And the day was a disappointment, for skies again were sullen in the dawn.

" All right," I called down, " don't turn out yet. It's a fair wind and lots of it ; we needn't get under way till seven."

Setting the alarm again, I turned in, and the racket and turmoil outside had faded in an instant ; I was sound asleep. Then, grudgingly at the appointed hour, we kicked away the blankets and yawned ourselves awake.

" Just a cup of coffee and a cold snack. It's too uncomfortable here for a regular breakfast."

"*You* think that too," he said, with a shade of relief in his voice, as he buttoned his oilskin.

We were soon on deck. The spacious region of our dream-world of last night had quite forgotten its character. After all that delicate allurement, the thing by daylight was distinctly matter-of-fact.

Flat land, tree-covered, was Mersea Island. Flat land, almost treeless, wide open marshes with a sandy shore, was Colne Point. The wind scoured over it all, and whistled; it cut the edges as with a knife, and made a pother of spume and breaking water everywhere on this little waste of sea.

The yacht buried herself as she turned to windward for the Bar Buoy. Wave after breaking wave was hit by her bows with a *thud*, and the spray swept aft in solid sheets. It rattled on our oilskins, dripped in rivulets, ran in streams. Then at the Bar Buoy, we bore away and ran before it, and the spray had ceased to fly.

"She plugs into it with pretty good conviction when you ask her," Robinson commented approvingly.

"She'll do all you want," I told him, "*as long as her gear holds*. But look aloft at her now; how many ropes are there, each board-tight and straining, and each playing its own part? If one rope parts with a crack, and a sail perhaps flops in the water, throwing her out of control, what then? Just where we are now, I had a mainsail slit clean across in something near a gale of wind. If she'd bumped on one of the shoals, I don't think she'd have survived the punishment that day."

"But it's not always so serious if something goes wrong?" he questioned, astutely enough, and I reassured him at once.

"It's a matter of sea-room. If there's lots of space, you can clear up the mess. But if you're being driven helplessly beamwise on to a shoal right beside you, the very moment you fall out of control, the danger is real. Look at the Goodwins," I added. "Vessels anchored in the Downs (in the old days of sail) dragged their anchors in heavy gales and went aground before there was time to get sail on them. If they'd only had sea-room they would never have been wrecked. It's just the same here."

Away we went, full before the wind, past Clacton and Walton. Harwich was soon in sight, but we were not entering, and course was shaped for Felixstowe and beyond.

"You remember last night?" I asked my companion. "Our gossip in the dark?"

"Shan't forget it *this* side." And he turned expectantly.

"We were seeing in fancy the old shipping" (and I winced at the crudity of my own phrase); "to-day we'll see with our own eyes a thirteenth-century haven, almost unchanged."

He watched me curiously as I bent a white-rimmed Union Jack on the signal-halliard. "What's that for?" he demanded.

"Fetch the pilot off. Pilot Jack, this."

We were nearly abreast of Shinglestreet in Suffolk, and were about to enter Orford Haven, bound for Aldeburgh.

"Forget the coastguard station," I told Robinson in a hurry, "it's not in the picture—wipe it out," for the station had taken up my signal on its flagstaff to pass it on to the pilot. "That's *not* the thirteenth century."

But the pilot himself was near enough to the old idea, as his sturdy boat tumbled in the steep waves. The yacht rounded up beside it, and a jerseyed figure redolent of salt-water was aboard with a swift skill born of long experience. His boat was soon trailing on a long painter astern.

"Dirty day to come up?" The pilot grinned as he took the tiller.

The waves were racing, foam-topped, shoreward, and breaking in a long line of foam upon the shingle-bank ahead. Not a sign or vestige of opening was visible. We seemed steering with headlong idiocy for the beach.

"Where *on earth?*" said Robinson, with his whimsical lift of eyebrows. "I suppose," he whispered, "the old thing with the earrings ain't drunk or lost his senses? You two know that there's a way." And he laughed. . . . "But I give it up; it's incredible."

The waves were breaking on both sides of us; we were in a turmoil of foam. One mighty heave and then another; the shingle was visible a few yards away, we could hear the pounding of the waves on it. And then we were in smooth water. We had entered the haven; a river had opened out, and ten miles of smooth passage, parallel with the sea, would take us past Orford to Aldeburgh.

This is a bar haven, quite unfit for deep-draught modern vessels, but it was admirably suited to the needs of the small shipping of the old centuries. With these wind-blown deserted shingle-banks, it is materially unchanged since the days of its prime, when it was the sea-gate of the quite prominent port of Orford. Just in this way the old Flemish carracks and Elizabethan traders would have entered.

" Seven-and-six, pilot ? "

" That's it, sir." He dropped into his own boat. " See you again when you're goin' out." And we let go his painter.

CHAPTER II

THE LOW SUFFOLK COAST-LINE

FROM shadow of the cabin the two of us emerged—into morning sunshine; and now, having swabbed the decks, we were indolently happy. We ought to have been below, cooking breakfast.

Two reefs down, yesterday we had sailed from Orford Haven back to Harwich and up the Orwell. It was an inconsequent method of exploration, doubling on our tracks like this; but here we were. We were anchored in the Orwell just above Shotley.

" Extraordinary, this keen air," my companion commented, " it's a regular inspiration. There's not a touch of cold, and yet it's . . ." He paused and sniffed appreciatively. The word was unwanted; his tone was enough. He looked across at the wooded landscape towards Pin Mill, flooded in sunshine, and the blue fairway.

" You fill the kettle, and I'll look after the frying-pan," I reminded him, and he came to earth with a laugh and a wry face.

. . . . . .

Then, in an hour or so, the yacht was stemming the flood-tide. At Landguard Point the mainsheet was hauled vigorously in, hand over hand.

" Belay it," I said in a hurry; Robinson did so;

and, when the sunlit mainsail went across, with a heavy *thud*, he saw the reason. " If you attempted to hold the rope in your hands," I explained, " you'd skin your palms." The story is told of a yachtsman, sailing alone, who had both his palms flayed in this way. Unable to handle his vessel himself, for it was sheer agony to touch a rope, he had to hoist signals of distress. A ruinous salvage bill from the fishermen who " rescued " him was the result.

" Lots of friction of course from a fast-running rope," my companion commented, and he felt the rough surface as he spoke.

He was right. Think of it, at its worst; only think, for instance, when a whaler has struck a great bull-whale. The whale sounds at once, and the line is whirling from the loggerhead, smoking from the heat, and a man throws water by the bucketful positively to prevent fire.

The yacht had left Landguard Point astern before the coastwise ebb came to befriend her. Felixstowe was abeam.

Not much of ancient Suffolk there, one might say perhaps, looking at the pier, hotels and terraced gardens. A seaside place is seldom seen at its best from the sea, and Felixstowe is not an exception. But the town is no modern upstart; true, it has sprung into size during recent years, but it has its own lineage and history. It was the " stowe " or dwelling of Felix of Burgundy, who introduced Christianity into East Anglia in days when history was so vague as to seem half mythical, and those grim long-boats were still haunting the seaboard. And solidly recorded when history became definite, it stood, and still stands, in the Domesday Book of the Conqueror: Fylchestowe or Fylstow, the name is written.

In sunlight we watched the low cliff, earth-coloured, slide by us. The yacht was slipping through a broken blue sea; she was rippling through it with a pleasant music—"travelling good tidily" would be the Suffolk phrase. Bawdsey Cliff, with the haven beside it, slid into the past, and Hollesley Bay was opened. In the long curve of coast lay Orford Haven. But not one ship was on the sea-line.

Isolated and primitive—this then was Suffolk. And the present glimpse was no unfair sample, for Suffolk seaways are deserted, and Suffolk havens have relapsed from business to quietude. The reason is twofold. In the first place, the sea has played havoc with them, and in the second the age of wooden ships has been superseded by that of iron.

"What's the sea done?" Robinson objected. "You said that Orford Haven was practically unchanged."

Perhaps I had over-stated my case the other day; the position of the entrance has probably altered, and possibly the two Bar Havens, both Orford and Bawdsey, were more accessible—being easier and deeper—in the early Middle Ages. The bars are now really obstructive. But the sea has also been busy elsewhere, and Orford and Bawdsey were by no means the only ports of Suffolk.

Where is Wadgate Haven, where the quays by Walton Castle, where is Dunwich? They harboured the ships of the Middle Ages, but the sea has overwhelmed them. They are drowned and gone. Where are the havens of Thorpe, Sizewell, Minsmere and Easton? The sea has retired and left

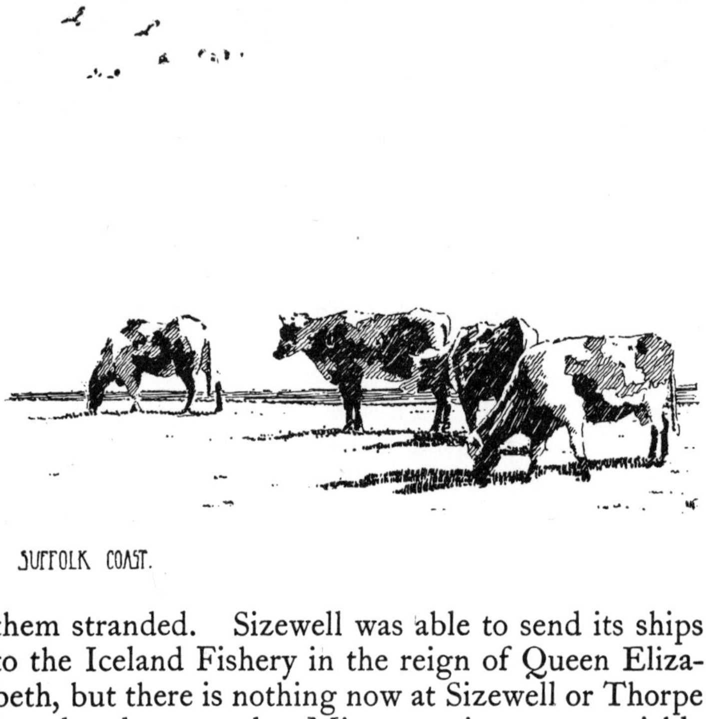

SUFFOLK COAST.

them stranded. Sizewell was able to send its ships to the Iceland Fishery in the reign of Queen Elizabeth, but there is nothing now at Sizewell or Thorpe but dry dusty sand. Minsmere is a petty trickle of river, and Easton an inland broad. Clearly, the sea has not busied itself in aid of the seaports of Suffolk. Some it has submerged and some forsaken.

Work at the helm was slack work to-day as she

lifted and dipped to the smooth swell. The wind was on our quarter.

One abiding natural haven the county possesses—Orwell Haven above Harwich. But natural havens have become of less account since the passing of sail; and waters where two hundred sail of ships have ridden safely in company in the old days are now empty. When ships were of wood, Suffolk built them; when they were under sail, she harboured them in her natural inlets. But now she builds them no longer, and the steamships neglect her more primitive havens, having business only with the artificial resources provided at Ipswich and Lowestoft.

Timber in Suffolk was plentiful, and Ipswich—in the reign of Henry VII—positively became the shipyard of London. The shipwrights' hammers were ringing at Woodbridge also, and at Orford, Aldeburgh and Walberswick. For more than a century Suffolk was industrially eminent. Then came decline, and, by a curious coincidence, it was a Suffolk man whose enterprise caused—in the long run—the ruin of Suffolk shipbuilding. Henry Johnson of Aldeburgh, in 1650 or thereabouts, founded the Blackwall Yard, which became the Thames Ironworks. London shipbuilding left Suffolk; and, with the introduction of iron, shipbuilding in the old yards has become merely a matter of history.

"So," I remarked to Robinson, as he swung his lissom white figure back into the cockpit after having slacked away the lee runner, "so there are more ghosts for you, more shadowy happenings along the grey sea-borders."

He looked up. "Ghosts?" he laughed. "It doesn't run to ghosts in full daylight. I got the fit on me the other night and talked rot. But . . . 'Not to-day, Baker'," he added, quoting an ancient Suffolk phrase which had caught his fancy.

Then his eye fell upon the small mop, hung just below the coaming. "And I tell you what," he added, "when we've next got the stoves going, I'm going to boil out that mop in soda. It's not fit to wash up with."

Then, for a season, we both were again intent upon the blue seaway, alive in sunlight.

"What about the ships at anchor? Where was it?" he asked, after an interval.

"Just literally here—for one place," I told him, while the sea lay empty about us. For Hollesley Bay was a favoured roadstead; protected by the coast and the Whiting Shoal, it was sheltered from all winds except north-east to east. Ships wind-bound have lain here by the hundred. Lowestoft and Yarmouth Roads, and Corton Road too, were important anchorages.

"Three-masters and two-masters, riding to their anchors. It's good to fancy it," he said, "and further out, I suppose, the ships bound t'other way, running free—with white canvas set, and white wake astern. . . . Yes, it makes a picture."

"The seascape was empty before they came, and it's empty now," I answered him. "Everything passes."

> " 'The generations of thy peers are fled
> And we ourselves shall go.' "

But he only smiled broadly; he even laughed. "Tears are a luxury I can't indulge this morning. Not the sobbing strain, it can't be done," he said.

"Let's set the jib-topsail," I decided, "she'll feel it, with this breeze."

He was alive at once, and had tumbled the white folds of sail out of the sail-locker with alacrity. Those quick fingers of his have a subtlety of touch which is obvious; with him, to handle a thing is to explore it. No man was ever less "all thumbs."

The jib-topsail of a yacht is not, like the other sails, set merely by means of ropes worked from the deck. It has first to be hooked on, by a series of hanks, to the topmast stay, which leads from the masthead to the end of the bowsprit. So, burdened with the long trailing sail, I clambered out to the bowsprit end. There one can cling and watch the broken foam at the cutwater. The water surged aft in a white stream unending. And I did my "hooking."

"Haul away," I shouted, as I clambered back. And up went the sail.

"That's simple enough," Robinson commented. "I'll do it next time. Useful practice."

"You can *get it in*, my laddie," I told him, "for that's much more amusing."

I explained. The setting of the sail is a comfortable matter because extra sails are only being hoisted when the wind is gentle and wants to be encouraged. More wind, in reason, is desired;

the sea is smooth. Then perhaps the wind does begin to breeze up, and the yacht delightedly responds, heeling appreciatively as she races through the water. But the wind pipes still more and even blusters a little, so that the sea is feeling it. There is too much wind for the topsails; she must be eased of them—and soon. She is hove to; and out you go. By this time she is pitching vigorously, and is inclined to stab each wave with her bowsprit; so that, when you have achieved your extreme station at the bowsprit end, you find yourself mixed up with the stabbing, being thrust bodily into each wave. It is sometimes as much as one can do to clutch on manfully for dear life, and at the same time subdue the flogging canvas. "One hand for the ship, but *always one for yourself*," was what the old sea-dogs said in the old-time windjammer; and it is good advice. There is also another point. Unless, on your return to deck, you wish to find your clothing wet from the waist downward, you had better strip to the buff beforehand. If the yacht is small and the sea at all rough, you had better strip. I speak from experience.

"Get mixed up in it, eh?" said Robinson; "all the better fun." And the yacht, almost level now with the entrance to Orford Haven, pointed her bowsprit still northward, and swayed graciously with every touch of breeze. There were those earth cliffs north of Bawdsey, now abeam, and then the coast flattened down to the long shingle-line, perioded by Martello towers:

"Where all beside is pebbly length of shore
And, far as eye can reach, it can discern no more."

"Suffolk coast then," Robinson reflected, picking up a lost train of thought from somewhere as he eyed the landfalls, "is pretty chock-full of romance and history. S'pose everywhere is," he added, "like London streets are, or anything else."

But really, as one explores them, one finds Suffolk

FROM BAWDSEY TO SHINGLESTREET

sea-borders interesting almost beyond the ordinary by reason of fluctuant fortunes. Lowestoft was a late comer among Suffolk seaports, and Ipswich alone has been consistently important. Woodbridge, Goseford, Orford, Aldeburgh and Dunwich have either disappeared or have ceased to rank as serious seaports at all. Yet, in the year of the Armada, it was the seaports now dead that contributed the ships of defence; the one ship contributed by Lowestoft (of 35 tons only) was contemptuously sent back, as of no value. Since then the whole face of things has so altered that, while Ipswich at one end of the county and Lowestoft at the other have kept pace with modern usages, the whole seaboard between them has become sequestered, a place merely of memories.

At moments we could hear the surf on the shingle-bank, as the yacht skimmed through the blue water close inshore. The tide was favouring her, "and she do go sweet, right in bore of the tide," as a smacksman said to me the other day.

The low shore-line yonder was adapted in the old years, not for sea-borne commerce only, but also for invasion. Ships of the invaders would be small, and Suffolk shores were open and vulnerable. When ships became larger, the danger from invasion was more than half dissipated—indeed a committee reporting in 1785 said that it seemed difficult for an enemy to make any attempt on this open coast.

We were standing close inshore. What Grenville Collins wrote in 1692 is still perfectly true. "You may sail from *Hosely Bay* down to the *Ness* all along the *Beach*, having good Sounding, you may turn down with safety."

Orfordness lighthouse was there on the sky-line. Alone it broke a blue horizon of inland Suffolk. Five miles to northward lay the town of Aldeburgh, like a vague blur on the flatness, and the shingle-bank was still uninterrupted. Away and away northward the yellow beach skirted.

The South Folk of East Anglia it was who bequeathed their name to the county. After them came the Danes; but the coast-line has since been

ORFORDNESS

" You may sail down to the Ness all along the Beach, having good sounding, you may turn down with safety." *Grenville Collins, 1602*

untroubled by way of regular invasion. The Flemings who landed, further south, in 1173 were not ordinary foreign invaders, being under command of an English Earl in insurrection against Henry II.

Even now the setting would fail little in appropriateness if some of those old tubs of mediæval shipping were really grounded inside the haven, or beached on the shingle. With ladders down the sides of the ships, men would be scrambling ashore —the sunlight flashing on axes and armour.

"All very pretty," Robinson objected, "but the invasions didn't come off."

"Raids did," I told him. In 1618 the author of the *Breviary of Suffolk* (after complaining that this coast "lyeth open and is ready for foreigne invasion, there bee so many havens, harbours, creekes and other places of ready discente") cited with evident feeling the "frequent proofe of the silly Dunkirkes who robbed our shores, came unto our havens and carried away our loden vessels." But the old writer remembered, with good philosophy, that raids are common to all seaboard shires, and "ought not to be reckoned as a particular incommoditie." A fear of invasion was always present; and the author of the *Breviary* invoked an unexpected line of defence. Invading armies, he said, discovering "our deep myrie soyle, our narrow and fowle lanes . . . *will have just cause to repent their rashnesse.*"

In times of danger they made "great use of Beacons neere the Sea-side," watched by horse and foot, and fired to pass the word—with their smoky

ORFORDNESS LIGHTHOUSE.

red flame—onward and inland. Reyce was writing only thirty years after the year of the Armada, and might again perhaps expect to see

> "Cape beyond cape, in endless range, those twinkling points of fire."

It can serve as one picture of bygone Suffolk. Another is the fleet actions with the Dutch, the tall ships in the smoke clouds, and the flames jumping. In 1665, some miles off Lowestoft, the English Fleet took eighteen Dutchmen and destroyed fourteen; but in 1672, in Sole Bay (off Southwold), we suffered heavily in a drawn battle.

The yacht reached onward toward Orfordness, where the tall lighthouse stood up, prominent and alone. Defoe called Orfordness "a noted point of land for the guide of the colliers and coasters,"

OFF LOWESTOFT, 3rd JUNE, 1665.

"THE TALL SHIPS IN THE SMOKE-CLOUDS, AND THE FLAMES JUMPING"

and described it—less authentically—as "a good shelter for them to ride under when a strong north-east wind blows and makes a foul shore on the coast." A lighthouse has been established on the point since 1792.

But now this day of ours was deteriorating; sunshine had gone, and grey cloud had robbed the world of its colour. Lunch was an interrupted function, for we were handing the topsails and getting the ship under snugger canvas.

"Grey North Sea," commented Robinson, and he reached for his oilskin. The North Sea responds with great swiftness to the moods of the weather, and we had already met it in some of its surly moments. Its steep seas in rough weather are more disconcerting to small craft than the longer waves of more spacious seaways. In the days of Queen Elizabeth it was reckoned as a severe school, producing sailors who had little more to learn in the way of hardship. Their old tag had it:

> "Wet and cold cannot make them shrink nor strain
> Whom the North Sea hath dyed in grain."

Its bleakness persists. Under the low sky of huddled grey cloud it had assumed a familiar aspect. Grey-green it heaved and topped, with increasing fringes of white—turbulent, fretful.

The rough shipmen of the Middle Ages, in their clumsy leewardly vessels, must have watched its moods with concern. And harsh weather was not their sole enemy. For piracy was rampant. It was a lucrative trade; and—even in the reign of

SAND DUNES AT THORPENESS

Queen Elizabeth—the pirates still had agents and informants in practically every port, who kept them posted as to the movements of vessels. Commissioners were appointed to suppress the traffic, but without avail.

Aldeburgh, in the greyness, lay abeam, a low line of houses on the shingly shore. Its life is now that of a mere seaside resort; its significance to the trade and enterprise of Suffolk has vanished. Lying on the "dead" coast, it is a useful example of the changed aspect of things. In 1590, Aldeburgh had 24 fishing boats of 20 tons, Walberswick and Dunwich had 7 each, Southwold 3, Lowestoft 2. *Now* Lowestoft has some 490 fishing vessels between 20 and 200 tons, and Aldeburgh none.

Aldeburgh was passed, and Thorpeness also. Thorpe is one of those lost havens of Suffolk; a small haven it used to possess, and in 1620 there was a beacon—placed probably to indicate the entrance. A little inland lake remains, and a cluster of seaside houses has sprung up beside it, dusty in the sand dunes. A few fishermen maintain their trade; with their beach boats they trawl inshore for plaice and sole, but their numbers lessen as the years go by.

Inshore of the buoy which marks Sizewell Bank the yacht shaped her course a-northward. The sandhills heap higher as they carry on to Sizewell Gap. Here, again, was once a port: in 1593, as already mentioned, Sizewell sent ships to the Iceland Fishery. The Beacon of "Syswell" was well known to mariners. There was a chapel for divine service as late as Queen Elizabeth's time, and "a considerable number of houses." Houses and port and fishing-boats have gone. For sheer aridity, little can rival the loose white sand of those dunes, sand that scatters, powdery and harsh, over everything. The deserted-looking cottages are white with it. The place is dry as a bone. Sea waves wash along a straight line of beach, unbroken by any inlet; the haven has vanished.

But years after the old town had gone, when its

SIZEWELL

ships and shipmen had long been shadows, there were nocturnal flittings here, real once more, upon that ghostly background. Fitzgerald wrote that he always had, "from a child, a mysterious feeling about that Sizewell Gap. There were reports of kegs of Hollands found under the Altar Cloth of Theberton Church near by, and we children looked with awe upon the Revenue Cutters which passed Aldbro', especially remembering one that went down with all hands, *The Ranger*." The midnight gangs, with their cutlasses and roped barrels, have ceased to haunt Sizewell; and the revenue cutters—no less than the ill-fated *Ranger*—have ceased to sail the sea. Sizewell remains alone, a second time deserted.

Smuggling had been rampant and unabashed along this coast-line in the eighteenth century. It amounted to a regular service. Partly the traffic was carried in small boats, but for the most part the vessels used were of 100 to 200 tons burden, swift ships, manned by sinister-looking fellows, quite as ready to fight authority as to evade it. Surprised in a small vessel by some heavily armed revenue cutter, they might "clap on Jackson," crowding every inch of "muslin" to make good their escape, but more often they were well prepared. And the whole shore-side population was in league. The gangs rode ashore fifty strong, while farm-labourers were paid a daily retaining fee to hold themselves in readiness, and a golden guinea for the night of the "run." In six months in 1745, over 4,500 horse-loads had been "run" in Suffolk.

The task of the Preventive officer was always a dangerous and thankless one; the marvel is that any recruits were obtained for it. In the eighteenth century the Customs officers accepted all the personal risks in return for their rather trifling pay; they were not entitled to pensions if disabled in the service, and no compensation was payable to their families if the men were killed. It is not surprising that they found means of supplementing their income. By law, all captured vessels ought to have been burnt; but, in practice, the officers would often enough seize the cargo only. Pocketing a handsome gratuity, they would look the other way while the vessel escaped.

But not only did authority traffic with smugglers in obscure transactions like these. During the Revolutionary and Napoleonic wars, the King's Government itself negotiated. Smugglers, with their moonlighting and their secret access to the opposite coast, were useful agents for the Intelligence Service; and the Government often protected them from prosecution for that reason.

Then the close of the wars brought drastic changes, for in 1818 the Coast Blockade was instituted. Overt smuggling was at an end; by trickery and evasion it managed to survive for a period, but every year the risks were sterner and the returns less adequate.

Yet another dead haven, a port stranded and desolate, was now abeam. Where Minsmere Level lies, Minsmere (or Mismore) Haven, shown on the old charts as a sizeable estuary, once opened. Its petty river now enters the sea, ditch-like, by a sluice. The whole coast-line is deserted.

We were leaving astern the broad levels, and the earth cliffs again heaped to a long mound above the grave of Dunwich.

By withdrawal or incursion the sea has indeed played havoc with the ports of Suffolk. But nowhere has it shown a grimmer mastery than here. A Roman settlement once, then the chief port of East Anglia in Saxon times, the chief port of Suffolk in the thirteenth century, and one of the chief ports of England, Dunwich had prospered. In the short space of seventy years the sea overran it, and the port was ruined. The sea-bed under our keel must be strewn with the ruin of a church and hall and wharf of the days of Edward I.

Our wind free, we had sailed by it. The cliffs had again fallen to that marsh level which Swinburne named " a land that is lonelier than ruin ":

> " Waste endless and boundless and flowerless,
> But of marsh blossoms fruitless as free,
> Where earth lies exhausted, as powerless
> To strive with the sea."

Past the entrance to the little harbour of Southwold we sailed. Between the twin harbour-piers we looked for a moment up the little creek that was the entrance to Dunwich quays and anchorage once; they closed, and we were passing Southwold town.

Through the grey sea the yacht drove; close inshore her course had been shaped and she thus obtained the protection of the coast-line. The low

COVEHITHE CHURCH

cliffs of Covehithe were again beside her, that "weather-shore" so valued by the old shipping when at anchor. But on this coast, as elsewhere, the fleets of anchored ships were often thrown into dire peril by some sudden shift of the storm wind. In the great storm of 1770, some thirty vessels were driven ashore on the sandbanks off Lowestoft—half of them went to pieces at once, and crews, to the number of some 2,000 all told, were drowned. The occurrence was among those which led to the movement in 1797 to establish the life-boat service of Great Britain.

Unmarked and unlighted, the shoals were—as always—a danger to navigation. There is no wide shoal-system, no complicated province like that of the Thames estuary, but a minor system off Lowestoft and Yarmouth has its own character and dangers.

LOWESTOFT TRAWLER; AND THE ANCIENT HERRING-FISHERY TOAST

Deep-water channels, narrow but adequate, run close in-shore of the shoals.

Lowestoft had the earliest light of the coast; in 1609 there was a single light, and in 1627 two lights were provided which, kept in line, led into the Stanford Channel. These two lights were "one for candle, and in the other a great fire made with coal." The first buoy, dating from 1621, marked a middle ground in Stanford Channel.

Here was Lowestoft. Kessingland and Pakefield had drifted by us in the grey evening, and the houses of Lowestoft, clustered along the shore-side, were close aboard. The twin light-houses on the harbour-arms were here, and the forest of masts, serried in the inner harbours, were vaguely seen. Town and harbour, all were crowded, congested, complex —a change after the simple quietude of the "dead" coast. Night was drawing on.

Blinking across the sea

LOWESTOFT

was the flash from Corton Light Vessel. Smith's Knoll and other trawling grounds (beside the famous Dogger Bank) lie to the north-eastward, and thus Corton is on the way home for the men of the trawlers. Thus the old rhyme said:

"When you come to Corton
The way begins to shorten."

In clouded dusk, deepening towards nightfall, the yacht had made her haven, and Lowestoft harbour, with its shifting lights and broken reflections, was quite magical in the late twilight, despite the leaden quality of sky and sea. There were voices from the darkness; a row-boat here or there crossed the greyness ; the water about us plash-plashed with a quiet rhythm. We were in harbour.

" No, let's keep away from all this modern business," said Robinson later, when he was getting drowsy. " It's that dead coast with all its ghosts and shadows, that's the coast that has the magic."

" Time for everything," I grunted ; and I dowsed the cabin light.

CHAPTER III

INTO SOUTHWOLD HARBOUR

WHITE in sunshine, a sea-gull hovered and dropped. Like a cork afloat, it was rocking on the water; again it spread its wings as the yacht streamed by it, full before the breeze. Our white furrow streaked the blueness as we drove.

"Fair wind, fine weather," I said appreciatively. The low shore-line was slipping away at speed.

"The birds fly all one way. Do you notice it?" I asked my companion. "They light and circle and rise, but their final drift is seaward."

He chose to be obtuse. "Don't see it," he yawned. "It sounds pretty enough; and got some pretty tale behind it?" His tone had a note of suspicion.

I said "perhaps," and I did not enlighten him. I kept it to myself. What I had really recalled was the figure of an old longshoreman, and a face sun-tanned and wrinkled. The old fellow had smiled as he spoke. "That looked mewsy (stormy), an' wind was dirty sou-easse. A rare bargain o' birds, hoverin' an' chatterin' roun' the brabble o' water down 'longside the shoal," he said. "You see 'em there, a-feedin'. Scour an' muck, they get it all, dirty feeders, though they look so clean-like. Then happen you look down again, an' all's clean

FLAT CALM

gone, feather an' bone. Bloke from the booms'l barge, loadin' gravel, he stood 'longside, him an' me lookin' out. 'Birds a-flyin' abroad, mate,' I said. Him, he grunted an' he sput, but he knowed no more'n a bull knows of a Sunday. 'That wind won't get out,' I told him. 'Get your hatches battened, mate; fair wind to-morrer.'"

And the same old fellow would expect, if the sea-birds flew landward, and he heard "the surf bark from nor'ard," to find the "wind abroad" before morning; a black north-easter would be booming full on shore, and the shingle-bank roaring.

"Ay," as he added, "an' sea nigh a breachin' ower it."

We had sailed northward past Corton to Gorleston in a light breeze, which flattened out completely, leaving us becalmed. Within sight of Yarmouth we lay motionless in the sunlight upon calm blue water; every rag of "muslin" had been set, but we did not move. Only the tide moved, slowly setting us northward still. The helm was handled, with a conscientious effort to keep her on some kind of course, but never a breath stirred, and not a touch of life was in her. Then, at the turn of the tide, an air sprang from northward; we decided to accept it, and run quietly down and make Southwold before dark.

The breeze freshened, and we were dropping the few miles comfortably astern.

"Look out for the nets." I said it too late, for we were among the "bowls," or little barrels used as floats for the warps of the nets. "We shall go over all right without fouling," I added, "we always do; but I'd rather keep clear when I can." One sometimes also sees a "dan," a small buoy with a flag, to show where fishing-lines have been shot. They toss lonely on the waves just now; but later on, a small boat will be headed this way. Talking broad Suffolk, the honest fellows who are descendants of Suffolk pirates and smugglers will be hauling at these warps, while their light boat rocks under them, lively enough if the wind is "abroad."

There is something intimately nautical about the movements of a man bred from boyhood to the sea. The instinct of him as he yields to the swing and tumble of the boat, his deft hand that makes fast a rope in one instant, immovably fast on a cleat, without even looking at it, the very glance which he bends aloft at his canvas or abroad to windward—every turn and touch betokens him. And the old lore of the sea is in him. The traditions of unlettered generations survive.

"Ay, that's a fair wind for you," that fisherman

might say, if he were to-day aboard with us. "Weather-shore all the way. Hark." A rugged finger might be lifted for silence, and we would strain our ears to attention as the yacht sailed steadfastly on. Every sound on board would be audible in the tense pause, the wash of the seas from her, and the creaking and strain of ropes. "Hark, there it is" (he would murmur); "*the sea calls to the wind*." Heard above the long wash-wash-wash of the seas about us, the voice of the surf along the distant beach would be blown, distinct and rhythmic. The wind is off-shore, and we are sheltered, in lee of the land. "The sea calls to the wind."

Evening was approaching: the sun was low in the sky. The time was one when "the gentleness of heaven is on the Sea." The seascape was suffused with last light, settling for the evenfall. Its blueness was less confident, becoming silvery and luminous. "Gentleness," Wordsworth's own description, was the only word.

For our light draught there would be ample water now. Wind and tide were comfortably balanced and the entrance would be easy. Pointed straight in from seaward at the north pier, the yacht would follow the line of the best water; with just sufficient wind in her sails to prevent the tide from setting her foul of the piles. So she carried on. She was in. The swift tide was sweeping her up the river. Into a recess, sheltered from run of the stream, she settled, and was comfortably warped up beside the stone wall.

SOUTHWOLD

We were moored. The long sea-line was visible over the sandhills on the Walberswick side, and the waves could be heard on the shore. The beach and harbour-piers were deserted, a few gulls in the distance were the sole life that stirred in the evening twilight. We brought our supper out to the cabin-top, and fed in the open.

This unfortunate harbour of Southwold has been a failure. The present harbour-piers were first erected in 1747. Two docks were then built, and the herring fishery was in full prosperity. But continual silt was the harbour's undoing. Even in the nineteenth century, thirteen times over it had to be cleared, again and yet again. And again and again the sand poured in and choked it. One last heroic effort was made to re-establish the old prosperity, but gradually the place again relapsed. The silted sand had won.

Such is the recent history of Southwold harbour, but the great days of its traffic were ended before those modern harbour-piers were thought of:

> "Swoule and Dunwich, and Walderswicke,
> All go in at one lousie creeke."

That is the old rhyme (ancient no doubt even in 1722) which Defoe attributed to the northern coasting seamen, "a rude verse of their own using, and I suppose of their own making." The entrance was one, but there were three separate branches. Grenville Collins thus described the harbour in 1692:

"*Dunwich*, *Walter-Swick* and *Sole*, or *Southwould*,

TWILIGHT AT BLYTHBURGH

go all in at one small creek, and divides into three Branches. *Dunwich* on the south Branch, *Sole* on the north, and *Walter-Swick* in the middle."

Reyce also, in 1618, says of the river Cockell (now Blyth) that "thus speeding to Blighborrow, it bequeathes it selfe into the bottome of the deep sea northward from Walderswick. So likewise into this haven do two other little brookes flow, the one coming southward from Dunwich, the other northward from Easton and Sowolde."

Defoe derides the notion that the "lousie creek" was once an important harbour. "This 'lousie creek,' in short" (he says), "is a little river at

A DESERTED WHARF ON THE BLYTH

Swoul, which our late famous atlas-maker calls a good harbour for ships, and rendezvous of the royal navy; but that by-the-bye; the author, it seems, knew no better."

But, *pace* Defoe, there seems little doubt that, in former centuries, the haven had been really important, and had once afforded "harbourage for men of war and ships of the largest burden." One must merely think back more deeply into the past. For this little deserted backwater of a place, where the yacht now lay solitary in the twilight, this humble ribbon of silted tide-way, is the sole remnant of the

ANCIENT RHYME ATTRIBUTED BY DEFOE TO
"THE NORTHERN COASTING SEAMEN"
INSET: ARMS OF SOUTHWOLD

proudest port of Suffolk. The ancient greatness of Dunwich is unquestioned. The three towns Dunwich, Southwold and Walberswick sent their shipping seaward through the one channel.

Evening had come. Only some solitary voice of a bird, far off, invaded the silence; and this silence brooded the more intimately for the tide beside us that "moving seemed asleep." The grey mystery of twilight was about us.

Half-reluctant to disenchant the stillness even with sound of oars, I at last pushed off in the dinghy, and crossed the few yards of water. On the smooth sand of the Walberswick shore I landed, and loitered afoot, aimless in the "moth-light." Though lamps began to wink from Walberswick windows, distant a short walk landward, there was a strange remoteness here. This solitary twilight was mine.

Walberswick is of great antiquity. In 1151 it had thirteen barques trading to Iceland, and its unrecorded shipping of earlier ages was doubtless equally important. It prospered—a place of business and enterprise.

But Dunwich, its great neighbour, overshadowed it almost to extinction. There Dunwich towered to southward, with monasteries, hospitals and churches, a walled and fortified town. "The strength thereof was terror and fear." In 1279 (in the reign of Edward I) Dunwich possessed "eighty great ships." Its "fayre shipps" were its pride, "which few townes in England had the like." When all the Cinque Ports and Yarmouth and Southampton were ordered to send one ship, Dun-

SOLE BAY, 28TH MAY, 1672

WALBERSWICK: FROM THE SHALLOWS OF THE RIVER BLYTH.

wich alone was ordered to send two. It was pre-eminent; its greatness brooked neither question nor denial.

Up past Walberswick sailed its "barkes" and "crayeurs," and the wharves teemed with traffic, while the barrelled masts and broad sails crowded the fairway.

Within seventy years the town had been ruined by the sea. In the first year of Edward III the old port was rendered entirely useless; twenty years later a great part of the town, with four hundred houses, was "drowned by the sea." Then, through the centuries, ruin succeeded ruin. In 1540 the church of St. John Baptist was taken down, and in the same century three chapels and two gates. In the reign of King Charles I "the foundation of the Temple buildings yielded to the irresistible force of the undermining surges," and—in 1667—on a night of terror for the inhabitants, the sea reached the market-place. In 1920 the tale was complete when, in an autumn storm, the ruin of the last of its six churches went down over the cliff. Dunwich has gone.

"Unlike those ruined cities" (as the old chronicler says) "whose fragments attest their former grandeur, Dunwich is wasted, desolate and void." Dunwich has gone.

Southwold, the other of the three towns, has also cowered under threat of the sea, but it survives. Quite wrongly, Southwold is often deemed late-born and upstart, in contrast with its picturesque fellows. The fact is not so. Southwold figures in the Domesday Book; it was Sudwolda then. Its church was founded in 1202, and the present building is said to date from Queen Mary's time. Later, in 1643, Cromwell's troopers were there, and they "brake down one hundred and thirty superstitious pictures and gave orders to take down 13 cherubims and to take down 20 angels." It has had its own variegated pages of history, both landward and seaward, for a thousand years.

Perhaps it owes its church to Queen Mary, but the sallow queen has another and more intimate memorial in the minds of men along the Suffolk country-side. "Thank God for a good fire and

A SHIP OF DUNWICH (LATE THIRTEENTH CENTURY)

nobody in it!" This is what the old-world peasant will still piously say when, some winter's night, he draws up his elbow-chair before the blazing hearth. "A good fire and nobody in it"—a grim memorial.

Fire on a wider scale has played its part in the history of Southwold-town. Both in 1596 and 1659

THE LAST OF DUNWICH
(DESTROYED BY ENCROACHMENT OF THE SEA
IN THE AUTUMN OF 1920)

Southwold suffered grievously, and on the latter occasion three-parts of the town, with the town hall, market hall, prison, warehouses and 238 dwelling-houses were consumed in four hours.

But I must return to my water-side. Alone in the nightfall, I had lingered by the rising tide-way, and watched the tide brimming continually, one creased and swirling current, direct and single. Landward, past the ruined staithes, it swam. There in the dusk were the boats drawn up on the shore-side, the little open luggers that are the only ships of the haven now.

Along the denes I turned back, seaward, and faced the full moon, just risen. It was red in the dusk. The path of gold on the sea—the " moon-way " as they say in Suffolk—was below it. Only the moon-way of gold betrayed the sea; neutral otherwise, it would have been lost in the haze.

The tide brimmed by, indifferently as when the old Dunwich traders entered, in days of the Plantagenets. The three towns which shared the common estuary were no peaceful compeers. They wrangled and fought throughout their history. They were for ever at each other's throats in the matter of receipt of harbour dues; they went to law with each other just as Ipswich and Harwich quarrelled on the Orwell. When Southwold was incorporated in the fourth year of Henry VII, the Act of Incorporation referred to "the many great variances and debates which had long time been had and continued" between them. Even until a hundred years ago the strife was at full tide. In 1829 a puncheon of whisky "found in the wash of the sea" or "grounded on shore" was pretext enough.

ON SOUTHWOLD BEACH

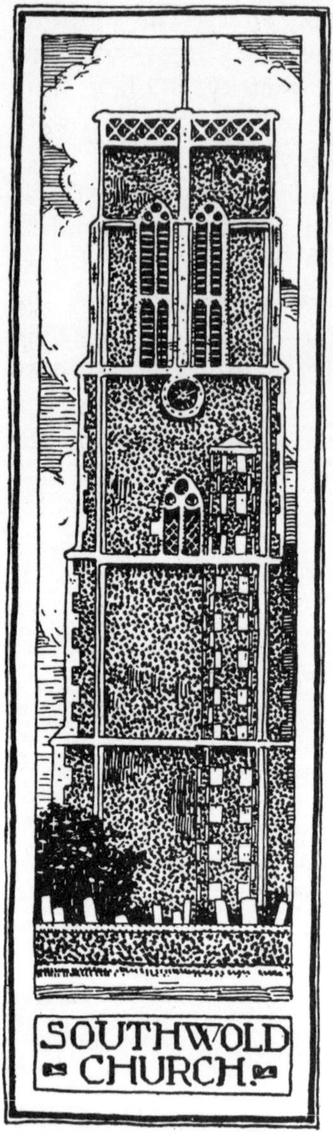

Dunwich and Southwold, both "notoriously litigious," went to law as to whether it was in the jurisdiction of one or the other, and Dunwich — although successful—had to pay its own costs of more than a thousand pounds.

Nor were these rivalries confined to threats and lawsuits. In days long past, methods were more direct. In the time of Edward III a Walberswick ship at Southwold was plundered by Dunwich men, and sixteen of the crew were murdered.

I had been gazing seaward, absorbed; and, like a ghost from the late twilight, Robinson was there. He had stolen on me unheard. Silent at my elbow he stood; and, with me, he gazed at the moon-way on the water.

"Well?" My question was hushed to a soft halftone, for speech seemed like an interruption somehow.

THE LITTLE WOODEN BRIDGE AT WALBERSWICK

"I came between the queer old houses and over the crazy little wooden bridge." He spoke barely above a mysterious whisper, just as one might begin a fairy-tale, "and . . ."

"The moonlight was on the little creeks, and the shore-line deserted," I went on in the same tone, taking the cue from him. "And under the moon, I saw the Dutchmen's topsails."

I could hear his breathing quicken, but he kept his face to the moonlight, and was silent.

"Then, as I watched, I knew them for our own sail of the line," I recited. "Smoke had blown from seaward all day.

'Well might you hear their guns, I guess,
From Sizewell Gap to Easton Ness.'

But silence had fallen now, and the ships passed like phantoms. . . ."

"Sole Bay, 1672. One can almost see them," said Robinson; and the spell was broken.

We paced along the shore-side, the waves breaking in the moonlight beside us; and we spoke of earlier Dutch wars, when the wounded were perpetually being landed along this coast, or when Blake himself was landed here, after action off the Gabbards in 1653, wounded, and "full of pain both in his head and left side, insomuch that he has no rest night or day, but continues groaning very sadly." And Dutchmen in their broad breeches, 2,000 prisoners from the Lowestoft battle, were landed here at Southwold—in 1665.

We had reached the harbour-pier on this southward side, and we paused. Moonlight glittered on the water between the piles, and the pier was black.

Walberswick . . . I

WALBERSWICK

was thinking, it goes back into history, with its barques of the twelfth century trading to Iceland and the North Sea. And the old ships would fit in with this setting to-night.

"Let's go for a sail in the dinghy," said Robinson, and, in that magical moonlight, we went.

. . . . .

Back on board, we lingered long before turning in. The mood of reverie was upon us both. Even after Dunwich had fallen, great ships were built here in Elizabethan and Stuart times. And earlier yet the place was a den of piracy, the whole countryside being in league with the grim sea-robbers. Industry, commerce, crime, battle—all have come this way; the old creek has been full of business, and has seen the vessels of all the long centuries, while the townships have done business in great waters. And nothing now, save the small beach-boats of the fishermen, remains.

" We're away early to-morrow," I yawned, " we must turn in." We went; we left the moonlight and the phantoms of history.

CHAPTER IV

NIGHT AND THE SEA OFF GOSEFORD

"ALMOST dark," my shipmate commented. The yacht was slipping quietly through the water as he spoke. He turned his eyes from the dull brown of sunset, trying to focus upon that blur of low coast-line. It had faded, lost beyond recognition.

Perhaps yachtsmen, like poets, are born, not made; and Robinson—though having missed the vocation hitherto—was certainly a born yachtsman.

"Take a little more mainsheet, wouldn't she?" he inquired. Yes, he was right; and the sheet was run out a trifle and belayed.

It was upon one of those evenings which abide in memory that the yacht had again rounded Orfordness, bound southward. A day, blue with the blueness of high summer, had softened into a mystery, the wind which had whipped the sea to foam-caps had become now a shadow of its former self. Twilight had fallen. The seascape, vigorous no longer, had been etherealised; the world was a world of shadows.

"Nice sort of time of day," my companion objected, "for entering an unlighted port through an awkward channel."

"We're not entering." I looked contentedly as I spoke at the evening star, a radiant point in the sober brownness of afterglow. Dusk had faded into night.

The vagrancy, the casual exploration, the uncertainties of cruising had, I knew, appealed to Robinson beyond anything that he had yet experienced, and it was a matter of pure indifference to him whether we made our way into some landlocked haven or not. Night was settling about us, and the sea was smooth.

"'After exceeding ill, a little good,'" I quoted. . . .

"No ills in this game, anyway," he replied, in a tone that had fallen mellow and drowsy. "Not one thing comes amiss," he continued. "An opinion after a mere week-end or two is a trifle fatuous perhaps," he apologised with that note of deprecation which is so mannerly, "but we're close up to naked fact at this game, and we begin to learn."

He paused, and I knew that he was casting about for words. An impression hovered; but he could not fix it. And, as I swayed the tiller, there sounded only, in the grey dusk, the ripple and the wash-wash-wash of our steady movement. I might have taxed him with those sturdy denials of his; he was now in that very vein which, by daylight, he so utterly disavowed. But I would not for the world.

The shape of him was blurred in the darkness. None the less, I could picture his clean-cut face

"IN DAYS THAT NEVER COME AGAIN."

intent on the west—"the last steps of day." I waited.

"*What* was the name of it?"

The question, apropos of nothing, was hardly explicit, but I guessed his new drift of thought. My account of that old Suffolk seaport that died without violence, that just faded out softly into a memory, had taken his imagination. The old town boasted its quays and shipping in its time, its sturdy shipmen and stout burgesses. It has gone, lost as the lost sunset of to-day.

"Goseford," I told him.

"Was it really there . . . or was it . . . is everything just a dream? It's just like echoes of a tune that haunt one, just like that feeling that baffled me the other night. I simply can't get a grip on reality, but I can believe any sort of eerie notion when we swim like this, poised in the twilight with everything shadowy and unreal. Excuse this rot I talk" (his hesitant voice was very low and musical), "forgive this utter rot, but the space and silence—it seems to get to my head like wine, and makes me feel sort of exultant, and say . . . well, I suppose most futile piffle."

His voice tailed off, and he was thinking. The yacht lifted faintly and dipped as she slid quietly through late summer dusk, "betwixt the gloaming and the murk."

"It was *there*," and he thrust out his head as if peering for the lost town in the nightfall. "It was there, with jolly-faced shipmen and wharves and old houses all askew. And the square-sailed ships

SETTING SAIL FOR SLUYS FROM WALTON (AT MOUTH OF THE DEBEN, SINCE SUBMERGED BY THE SEA)

went out and in. Fellows hauling on the ropes, and capstans creaking . . . laughter and voices over the water. And what I feel is—this." He paused again, feeling for his words. "Nothing is fixed, everything flows and changes—the very earth was vague and misty once, and all the light and colour of the world still moves in one long pageant, never stopping. *Or do we fancy them all?* Are they a phantom—things like the pictures of a magic-lantern, things full of light and colour, and yet really—*not there at all?*

I waited, silent; but his own silence became fixed and stubborn. He was half ashamed of his burst of confidence, and of ideas which had sounded (as these things will) so crude and unlikely when reduced to common words. He knew nothing (for I asked him afterwards) of Plato's fancy of humanity as prisoners in a dark cave, forced by their fetters to look at a dead wall in front of them, so that they cannot see the light behind them or the objects that pass in the open. *They only see the shadows of those objects and of themselves in the dead wall, and take those shadows for reality.*

The whole company of dreamers and of philosophers who have groped among shadows were his fellows and kinsmen.

"I deny nothing," I told him. "Yet I fancy that, if we see the light to-morrow, we'll find a shore of sand and pebbles there, and tufted grasses, and a cluster of modern cottages. Except for the occasional yacht or barge there's no shipping. Of course we *might* wake up in the thirteenth century, and see the broad-bellied sailing-tubs and the hooded shipmen. But I don't fancy we shall; the chances are somehow against it."

He sighed deeply, and then he laughed.

"Of course," he said briskly, "and yet . . ." He hesitated again, so that I guessed, or fancied that I had guessed, the sensation that troubled him.

"A warmth within the breast would melt
The freezing reason's colder part,
And like a man in wrath the heart
Stood up and answer'd 'I have felt.'"

He had felt the neighbourhood of subtler realities. Dawn might again to-morrow bring the commonplace, but he stood convicted just now that the veriest shadows are as real as the facts of day.

"Yes, yes . . ." he added, and laughed. "I s'pose I'm waking up." And he rubbed his eyes.

He watched me as I swayed the tiller; and, turning, he looked up at the mainsail, dark in the night.

"The breeze still holds," he said. "Where are we?"

He glanced approvingly over the quarter as he asked the question, and we watched the long patterns of bubbles strung out at leisurely pace that drifted into darkness astern. Quiet though the nightfall was, we were not becalmed; the tide was with us, and the yacht was slipping through it, adding her own smooth progress to that silent movement of tide.

"We'll stand moderately close inshore," I told him. "Inside the Cutler shoal we're out of the track of the shipping—here in the red sector of Orfordness Light. When we're reasonably close to the haven entrance we may as well let go—somewhere off the seamark."

The seamark would not materialise to-night, although the loom of the land might be visible. But there was no doubt. Night was now undisputed; a certain wanness on the west held the last shadow of day, subdued to a vestige, a glimmer. The stars were above us.

So, in this world of shadow we could steal onward; or, if so minded, here we could pause. We had only to let go the anchor. Gradually the yacht, rounded to meet the tide, would strain her cable tight; and the smooth tidal current—moving the whole body of water southward—would sweep, with a quiet clutter and chuckle unending, past her bows.

"What about it?" I said. "Ready to turn in?"

We anchored.

The sails had been furled, the tiller lashed, and the riding-light hung in the forestay. She lifted and rocked with her easy buoyancy, and the soft wind sighed in the darkness. I lingered on deck, loth to leave that space and serenity. Reluctantly, at long last, I turned in.

The lamplight of the cabin, homely always and warm, was a contrast as I entered. Then, at full length on my bunk, I felt the lift and heave of each wave that swelled smoothly shoreward under us.

"'Rocked in the cradle of the deep,'"

Robinson quoted drowsily from the bunk opposite, and, upon that note, we relaxed our hold on everything. Slumber took us.

Any added severity of movement, from high wind and rougher sea, would awaken me, I knew. Orfordness Light on one side, and the recurrent flash of the Cork Light Vessel on the other, would give us our bearings in an instant if we had to tumble up,

SHIPS OF GOSEFORD
(INSCRIPTION FROM FROISSART, 1340)

sleep-heavy, into the darkness and driven spray, and to clear out in a hurry during the night.

But there was no such necessity. We were rocked in that cradle with a motion faultlessly even. Even and unbroken it continued all night; the stars were above us, and we slept. Gradually in the east to seaward the dawn must have quickened, with a slow luminous quality warming into red sunrise and killing the starshine, but we saw nothing of it all. We slept.

The slow rhythm was still the same when our eyes opened to full daylight and to shafts of sunlight golden across the cabin. One looked ou't appreciatively. There was the seamark just opposite to us on brown cliffs; the sea's face was blue, and away to the south-westward clustered the roofs of the hamlet at Felixstowe ferry. An easterly breeze was keeping the sea alert in the sunshine.

True enough, we had awakened in the twentieth century and not the thirteenth. The dozen roofs on the low shore could claim no likeness to a port the equal of Ipswich, and greater than Lowestoft or Yarmouth, places then unknown. The coast-line was empty and deserted, no traffic, no industry.

Yet Goseford, the very name of which has perished, was wont to contribute its own vessels for the needs of the Crown. When, in 1342, there was a call upon the ports of Suffolk for shipping for the expedition of Sir Walter Manny to France, Ipswich sent 14 vessels, Goseford 15, Dunwich 4, and Orford 1. And Goseford had its own vigorous race of shipmen, who traded abroad, and were ready enough for lawlessness and violence. In 1310 the crew of a Goseford ship at La Rochelle boarded and ransacked an anchored vessel in rank open piracy. In and out of the harbour, with their painted shields and bannered sails, the ships of Goseford plied.

Perhaps—as already said—the bar has shoaled. But it has changed little during the past two hundred years at all events; and the description given by Grenville Collins still holds good; the harbour "Lyeth just at the west end of *Balsey-Cliff* and is a Bar-Haven, which is but three or four foot water at low water." Between those shingle-banks the ornate and square-rigged shipping of King Charles II entered, and a century earlier, the Queen's ship

Vanguard, at time of the Armada, came in search of the enemy as far as " Bedsey-Cliff," that same cliff to northward of the haven. She then turned back again and provisioned at Harwich, for the Armada was already in flight.

But now? Well, we had awakened in the twentieth century; sunlight was golden, and the breeze was light, easterly.

CHAPTER V

ENTERING BAWDSEY HAVEN

ROBINSON had appeared again on deck, matter-of-fact, his face shining from the towel. He had had a swim and a shave. We were still at anchor about a mile off-shore, opposite the seamark on Bawdsey Cliff; we intended to enter the haven with this morning's tide. He now focussed his binoculars on the little hamlet.

" You didn't overdo the desolation," he admitted. " No port and no shipping. Just a ' pub ' for the pilots to sit in, I suppose, waiting for the job that doesn't come along."

The haven still supports a couple of pilots, for a few barges trade in and out for Woodbridge, and there are the casual yachts.

It is not a straightforward place to enter. The channel is narrow, being hemmed by sunken shingle-banks. They jut out from shore on either side of it, and their position at high water is marked only by the fringe of surf. The Admiralty Pilot Book insists that local assistance is essential, " as the bar and shoals are subject to change," and " the tides are exceedingly strong at the entrance."

That swift tide bears its own part in the shifting of the bar and shoals. When a strong body of water, ebbing seaward at six or seven knots, meets, head-on, the shoreward breakers of a south-easterly gale, then there is Bedlam let loose. Among the shingle-banks it is a foam-spattered confusion unspeakable. The shingle-mounds, under the drive and suck of it, are hollowed or heaped as the water wills. Valleys are made into mountains, and the hills laid low. The pilots can go off duty while the turmoil continues, for no ship could enter save as the driftwood of a total wreck.

But when the storm is over the pilots are again busy. They are in their boats, surveying and sounding with the utmost care; they are finding where the changed course of the fairway now enters.

There are leading-marks on shore which should be kept in line. These are moved from time to time by the pilots as the channel changes. It cannot be assumed that strict alignment will give the best water, for the pilots often rely upon other marks as well for their own work; but—generally speaking—if the stranger, keeping clear of the shoal to westward, is able to get the marks in line at the right spot, keep them there until within fifty yards of the shore just west of the Martello tower, and then turn westward, keeping the shore aboard, in he will go.

"It sounds perfectly simple—on paper," I told Robinson, "and it probably offers no difficulty to anyone often in and out. But I confess that things are apt to look oddly unfamiliar after the absence of a year or two."

That is the trouble. One strains one's eyes to

identify a landmark or leading-mark, but the tidal mill-race does not tarry. In it sweeps over shallow places and deep with swift indifference.

My shipmate looked up at the cloudless sky, and then at the sea around us. The light breeze was constant and true.

"I know what you're thinking," I said. "A fine morning to miss the pilot. So we will."

We were just sweating up the main halliards, making sail. "Bravo," he said.

"Mind you," I went on, as I belayed and began to coil down, "mind you, I only do it because failure won't make us pay any forfeit. There'll be no breaking seas. I don't suppose she'll take much harm if we do miss the channel and touch. The tide will take her in somehow."

So we laid our course for the entrance. In charge, I handled the tiller with anxiety. Conditions were excellent; but the tides were at springs, and the pace was headlong. With one eye on the channel and one shoreward, trying to spot the leading-marks, I steered her, and she swept on. Wooden breakwaters, and cottages, and telegraph poles were sliding horizontally past us as if they were on wheels, well-oiled and noiseless. There was Bawdsey Ferry ahead; and the anchorage, full of small vessels, was beyond it. She was sweeping in, full-tilt; she had nearly done it. The shingle-bank to southward was slipping healthily past.

Then—*scrunch*, and then a dead stop. With confounded perversity, when almost through she was fast aground. The water was racing past her, and

· AT · BAWDSEY · HAVEN. ·

the waves were breaking, with a *splash* and a *splash* and a *splash*, on her stern. I had piled her up.

"Get everything off her," I growled, in response to Robinson's look of inquiry, for the sails were only driving her further aground. Then I dropped overboard into the dinghy, taking the lead-line with me, in order to locate the true channel. There was not a great deal of water anywhere, but I found the best of it and laid out the kedge-anchor with a long warp.

The yacht was bump-bumping on the shingle in a manner that gave one a twinge of evil conscience. Kedges are apt to drag. Pulling manfully on his rope, the mariner feels the dead resistance succumb; hand over hand the rope comes in. "Kedge coming home," he knows it; for the yacht has not stirred.

ENTRANCE TO BAWDSEY HAVEN

" Moving, is she ? " I asked, as I hauled slowly on the warp.

Yes ; the gallant little kedge had bitten truly in the channel-bed, the rope was held as firmly as any bollard on a harbour wall could hold it. The bump-bump-bumping was over ; she rode smoothly—afloat.

But it was one thing to have her afloat and quite another to get her under control in so narrow a gut before she had time to ground again.

The expedient followed was simple. I passed the kedge-warp aft, and turned the yacht's bows landward, on course. Then I hauled gradually in over the stern, while my shipmate stood, foresail-halliard in hand, ready to run the sail up immediately I shouted that the kedge had broken.

" That ain't a mite o' use, a-haulin' same's that ; you won't never get her off ; not that way, you won't. You want that warp o' yourn ower the *bows*."

Robinson looked round, with a laughable air of amazed resentment.

Boats had, as is usual on these occasions, sprung up around our discomfited vessel, and several appreciative shellbacks were there—a critical audience. The grizzled speaker, after delivering judgment, spat into the water and then replaced his pipe between mahogany lips. He had anchored his boat in order to watch the better.

After casting one swift glance at my own unperturbed labours, Robinson turned to the offender.

"You go and boil yourself," he retorted. But there was a geniality of tone which robbed the rejoinder of offence. And, over the stern, I still hauled away.

"Kedge broken. Up fores'l."

On tiptoe of expectation I watched her. She gathered way. "Up main." And as the peak swung outboard and the sail filled, she sent the white bubbles by the thousand along that blue water astern; she was past the ferry, and had entered Deben river.

"Well, tha'ss a rum 'un," perhaps the old fellow said. We had escaped him. Dwindling to stern of us were the breakwaters and boats, under a receding blue horizon; and over the bowsprit now were the green fields and the farmsteads of Suffolk.

The tidal flats lay still uncovered. Water-smoothed and monotonous, they bordered the solid bank. In shallows, the herons here and there stood sentinel, and wild-duck scattered

AT FELIXSTOWE FERRY

BARGE ENTERING BAWDSEY HAVEN

and flew. This was the Deben.

It was afternoon when, having returned and anchored the yacht comfortably beside the Ferry, we went ashore. We paced up the low cliff towards Felixstowe.

From the cliffs the position of the shoals is clear enough. Twin lines of broken white water stretch seaward, on either side the channel, with the precision and straightness of piers. Between them, when the bar is well flooded, lies the fairway.

"Only it ain't quite so straightforward-like, down there knocked about in the paffle, tumblin' about like a little boat will." An old boatman trudged beside us as we returned towards the haven, and chatted genially on the way. "A bloke, he come in here, and he didn't make no 'count for the bar. Come smellin' in, like, not tide-time proper, and he see the waves a-breakin' right acrost him. Down-hellum in a hurry, *he* did, and beat away seaward. An' right he was too."

We had expected at least some uncomfortable happening, even a full shipwreck. But we were disappointed of both. It even transpired that the "bloke," an old salt himself, had negotiated the entrance later on without local assistance. The story therefore failed to point any obvious moral. I could indeed have bettered it myself—but I forbore.

Anyone who has seen the bar in a strong blow will appreciate the boatman's comment. The wind on one occasion had swept up strongly from the south'ard and had reached gale-force. The yacht rocked in the haven, secure, while the gale was making a rabid seaway outside. As I lay awake that night in the cabin, the gale swung in thunder overhead, and the whole air was loud with it. Between gusts, as if taking breath for a lustier effort, it momentarily would lull. Grandly, through the pause, roared the waves on the shingle-banks outside. Then, with a shriek and a whistle, the louder wind was again in command.

With daylight the gale was moderating, and the hoarse voice of the surf had become continuous.

Shadows from the houses and from the Martello tower were longer, and the sunlight was golden, as we returned to the open grassy spaces and the shingle beach. Our previous companion had shaped course towards some tarred sheds, and here, at the water-side, we met the pilot pacing meditatively, pipe in mouth.

"Nice little haven," he said, setting his feet apart and looking seaward, "only wants knowin', o' course, same's most things do. Tidy little haven for them as knows, only it don't carry no shippin', not like it used to."

"There are the barges still, up and down to Woodbridge," I reminded him.

"Vessels there were, old-times, out by that there buoy yonder, waitin' water to come in. Lots on 'em. And *berges?*" he continued, with a note of challenge. "Berges, up an' down now? I've known *eighty-four* berges come in the haven in one month when the ole cement works was up at Waldringfield. No, no, not much doin' now, beggared there ain't."

He shook his head ruefully. "Yes, them ole berges, in an' out, they kep' us alive-like. Sailin' 'em or dredgin' 'em, all one to us. In an' out they come, no end on 'em. Any ole time, it's all one to us; know this little ole haven? Rum 'un if we didn't." And he sighed at thought of glories faded.

The process of "dredgin'," to which he referred, has no relation to deepening the river-bottom. It is quite a different business, though the name is identical. The ship's sails are furled, and her anchor is let go, but the amount of chain paid out is insufficient to let the anchor bite. The vessel still drifts, but the anchor dragging along the bottom retards her, and makes her speed of drift less than the speed of the tide. She is thus given (reverse) steerage-way, and the helmsman can direct her.

BAWDSEY HAVEN

The process can be witnessed any day on the River Thames, where bargemen often negotiate bridges in this manner.

The pilot's eye was always seaward, and he had observed a yawl that was shaping course for the haven. His interest was quite detached, that of spectator, although she was fast approaching shallow water and was signalling for a pilot. There was not yet enough water on the bar. Suddenly she luffed and hung ashake and then filled and turned seaward again.

" Tha'ss better," he cackled, " you got to wait." He had made no sign to warn her. " You got to wait. Stan' off an' on, an hour an' more, you got to, yet," he added.

In the evening sunlight, we dragged our dinghy—grating over the shingle—to the water's edge.

" Come on," said Robinson, " here's the egg-box, and—catch ! "—this was the bread-sack—" no breakables." We had been shopping in Felixstowe.

We pulled out to the yacht. It was early twilight when we again emerged, dinner having been cleared ; and that yacht which had been standing off and on had just entered the haven.

" Wonderful evening," my shipmate had said ; and the beauty of it absorbed us and made us silent as we washed up the crockery. The sky was a blur of gold to westward, and night was rising, ghost-like, from the sea.

That grey sea beyond the bar is over the dead. If entering the haven from the southward, a ship must sail over the dim ruin of a lost Atlantis. In

" the purple twilights under the sea " may still perhaps be found the ghosts of men and shadows of the sunken stronghold. Seaward of Felixstowe ferry, the Roman castle of Walton once stood guardian against the raiding ships of the Saxon. Those walls, bound with mortar not less hard than the stone itself, were proof against the storms of a thousand years; they stood, bluff and mighty, long after the Saxons had over-swept the land and the Roman had become a legend. In Walton Castle, in 1338, Edward III lodged royally just before he sailed for France in the campaign of Creçy. Above the scarred walls, even then ancient, the banners floated; and under shelter of the Castle lay its own harbour, Wadgate Haven, crowded no doubt with the barrelled masts of mediæval shipping. The sea has overwhelmed everything. Not a trace remains; Walton has vanished.

. . . . .

" This late daylight gives us almost too little of the night," one of us said, for the night has its own charm and mystery.

" It's bedtime now, *whateffer*," was Robinson's verdict. And once more we left the space and wonder of it all.

CHAPTER VI

HIGH AND DRY AT WOODBRIDGE

THE name of Fitzgerald was inevitable when Woodbridge was mentioned.

"Omar Khayyám?" said Robinson, and he paused, sea-booted and bucket in hand, from his swabbing of the decks. "A stout fellow was Omar.

> 'Unborn To-Morrow and dead Yesterday,
> Why fret about them if To-day be sweet?'"

he quoted, pensively. Then he put down the bucket. "And this is good enough for a start," he admitted. "'*To-day*,' Omar's 'To-day,' it's a marvellous fact."

The breadth of open seaways had faded out of our picture, for yesterday the shingle-banks spread long arms astern of us, intercepting the view. That bare sea-horizon had vanished; the yacht was in Deben River, and here she had anchored.

With her gentler setting of hill and meadow, this placid day was "soft and tunable." And the mood of the country-side was at one also, a single quietude possessed everything. The yacht had now again swung with change of tide, for the young flood had begun to slip stealthily landward, and she would soon be bound up-stream with it—to the old town of Woodbridge, to ancient Woodbridge, a town well known before the Conquest and great in the Middle Ages.

"More dead seaports?" Robinson, who was fidgeting with the jib traveller, looked up with that whimsical smile of his. "Never a ship to trouble it, it's gone to sleep properly."

He was in a restless mood, chafing because the wind was light. "Almost as dead as Woodbridge," he laughed, a little abashed (or so I fancied) at levity in the face of the dead centuries.

"Almost," I answered, as I spread out our drying cloth after the washing-up. "But 'dead' isn't perhaps the exact note in the case of Woodbridge. It's more like some old vessel left dry by the tide, stranded." Things have simply gone away and left it: industry, trade, deep-water and all—all have gone and left the old place forsaken.

"Let's go and see for ourselves," he said. His fingers were on the gaskets of the mainsail, and I knew that his sole longing was to get the sails on her and break out that anchor. I need not longer gainsay him; the tide would serve. We made sail.

. . . . .

Woodbridge, old-fashioned and unpretending, was a fit haunt for the figure of Fitzgerald, and he was twenty years familiar with the slow life of the Deben. When old friends were dead, and new vandals defacing the country-side of England, then it was that he would "get to the water, where Friends are not buried, nor Pathways stopt up."

It was in 1860—then in middle life—that he came to Woodbridge. He had a small yacht built which

HIGH WATER AT WOODBRIDGE·

he called *The Scandal*, naming it—he said—after the main staple of Woodbridge. "All other possible names" (he added) "had been used up."

Woodbridge—true enough—has not the traffic in more reputable commodities which it once enjoyed. In the reign of King James I, for instance, Woodbridge "was richer than Yarmouth and all its members combined." It had its own ships (in 1634 it possessed seventeen vessels of 100 to 300 tons), and its own foreign trade. All has gone.

Fitzgerald sailed about the Suffolk waters with his skipper Newson. Newson carried his head perched to one side. "Like a magpie looking in a quart-pot," said Fitzgerald, and added, "He is always smiling, yet the wretched fellow is the father of twins."

Afloat with Newson and others Fitzgerald was content enough:

"I am happiest going in my little Boat round the coast to Aldbro', with some Bottled Porter and some Bread and Cheese, and some good rough Soul who works the Boat and chews his Tobacco in peace. An Aldbro' Sailor talking of my boat said: 'She go like a Wiolin, she do!' What a pretty conceit, is it not? As the Bow slides over the Strings in a liquid Tune. Another man was talking yesterday of a great Storm: 'and, in a moment, all as calm as a Clock.'"

On Fitzgerald's own waters, the yacht to-day slipped quietly up from Bawdsey Haven with the tide. The wind was fair: between tide-forsaken flats she wound her way, and the fields folded more closely upon her as she made landward. Wind-swept levels were exchanged for slope and wooded hill. By a channel always narrowing she glided; imaged in smooth water, she stirred the reflections with the ripple of her course; then—off Woodbridge, close beside the town—she let go her anchor. Broken reflections re-settled, and she slept in sunlight, harmonised with drowsy town and sleeping landscape.

Woodbridge has fallen out of the race, it has resigned its hopes. Even a century ago the town was a living competitor, but the cause of its inevitable decline was recognised. "The only port likely to compete with Ipswich is kept down" (said a writer of the time), "in her energies to become something better than she is at present, by the shallow waters and other unconquerable obstacles of her river." That was her trouble.

While one lingers about the quiet waterside at Woodbridge, the past is oddly unreal. To us of modern years, accustomed to see Nature evicted by industry, this return of hers is hardly credible. Not less difficult it is—standing in London traffic—to picture the marsh-bordered solitude that once was there than to see this quiet waterside as a place of stirring business.

Woodbridge of the far-away years with its shipyards and docks has gone. Ships of 200 tons burden were built here when such ships were great vessels in the eyes of men. Early in the days of Queen Elizabeth this busy port was a close rival to Ipswich; then, between 1625 and 1638, a Levant merchant-ship of 400 tons, the largest Suffolk ship of her time, was launched here. But decline had already set in, for the size of ships was increasing, and Woodbridge Bar was shoaling. It was a place for first-rates no longer. Between 1650 and 1675, five fourth-rates were built; King's ships, splendidly carved and begilt, they sailed seaward and were gone. They left Woodbridge, stranded behind its shoaling bar, a place reduced and soon forgotten. The swallows now skim about forsaken fields that once were shipyards.

We were talking of it, and Robinson threw in an astute objection.

Levant Merchant Ship built at Woodbridge circa 1625

"The Bar stopped building of ships beyond a certain draught," he said. "I can understand that; but it didn't kill trade." He glanced over at the railway station, close to the waterside, as he spoke. "Until the railway came, water-borne traffic was cheapest. Surely. Small craft, and so on."

He was perfectly right. Long after its eclipse as a shipbuilding town Woodbridge had considerable commercial activity by water. Defoe mentions the town as the chief port for exporting Suffolk butter; barrelled and pickled in casks, it was even sent to the West Indies. *The Suffolk Traveller* refers to the regular London traders that sailed to and from the port, and speaks of other vessels engaged in the Newcastle and Sunderland trade. In 1692 there were "nine or ten hoys to and from London weekly." But the railway has since taken the trade. Save for the few spritsail barges that casually wander up to Woodbridge, the whole water-borne trade has passed away.

At high water there is a lake-like stretch of water, which dwindles with the ebb to a poor trickle across the tidal mud. It was now high tide, and the place was presentable; we loitered in sunshine before returning on board.

Then unhurriedly, as befitted so genial a day, we settled ourselves in the dinghy and pulled away back to the yacht. We were outward bound. The water, wind-rippled, was alive, for a breeze had sprung from seaward. White clouds were deepening the blue.

"Odd name—'Woodbridge,' when it hasn't got a bridge," Robinson commented. He was gazing at the green marshland opposite, where cloud-shadows chased one another. "Can't get there direct except by ferry, I suppose? *Was* there a bridge?"

The name has been a problem to more people than ourselves, for various explanations have been offered. In some modern books it is solemnly suggested that Woodbridge owes its name to a wooden bridge over a hollow between two parks. But the idea is scouted by serious writers. In days of the Confessor the place was known as Udelsbruge, and the name appears in the Domesday Book as Udebryge. In the reign of Henry VII it was Wodebrigg. Etymology must be left to those who are sufficient for these things, but it appears that the name possibly represents Woden's Bury or Town, and that it has no real connection with bridges at all.

Nevertheless, a bridge over the river there must have been—whether the one still existing at Melton or a vanished one nearer the town, for we find it mentioned in 1618 in the list of bridges over the "Deane": viz. "by Woodbridge."

The yacht would be compelled to win seaward by beating; so up went the sails and away she flew, heeling from the breeze, with quick curve and recover at the end of each short tack. It was really an ill-chosen time for departure—at extreme top of the tide, with water deceptively blue, over mud-bank and fairway alike. The deep channel curves and twists, and there is a sad frugality in the matter of withies.

"Lee Ho"—Woodbridge was now well astern, and opposite Kingston Quay were two withies which appeared to be "doubles," one each side of the channel. Without a flicker of hesitation I obeyed them, and laid course accordingly.

"*Hul*-lo." She was on. Her sunlit sails still bellied with the wind, but her white wake had vanished, and she was immovably fast.

On a falling tide it was matter for instant action. Unless shifted at once, she would not float again until next high water. With swift decision I laid my plans and we made our one bid for escape by laying out the kedge; she shifted a little but re-settled at once; it was a lost throw. *J'y suis,*

SUFFOLK HOY, 1692, TRADING BETWEEN WOODBRIDGE AND LONDON

j'y reste. Here we should be until to-morrow morning.

Perfectly snug, as if in a cradle moulded to her shape, she lay, with the soft mud pressing about her hull, and holding her almost upright. There was no fear of damage to the yacht, the question was merely one of delay and indignity. The ebb-tide streamed away seaward; the channel narrowed and drew itself virtuously apart, disclosing the measure of our defection; and here she lay, tide-forsaken. She sat forlorn upon this water-rounded surface of ooze. A deep gash, furrowing the mud deeply astern of her, was evidence of our misdirected progress.

Sometimes by accident, and sometimes by design, I have "dried out" in tidal waters like this. Islanded in the ooze, with its blue pools and changing bird-life, the situation has its own pleasures. But to-day one guilty thought darkened the horizon. Reference to the Nautical Almanac had told me that the tides were "taking off"; there would be less depth to-morrow than to-day, and we had sailed her on hard, right at top of the tide. Should we escape?

The morrow would show, and sufficient unto the day is the evil thereof. For the present we were responsible only to make every preparation.

Robinson was alive with interest and expectation, for this was his first real experience of the kind.

"What now?" he demanded, "nothing to be done till she floats?"

True, we could not actually pull her off until then, but it was necessary to think out our plans

FORSAKEN BY THE TIDE.

THE SHALLOWS OF THE DEBEN

and to have everything cut and dried. The extreme of high water does not last long, maybe only a few minutes. And the moment is then or not at all.

Along that track of hers in the mud, a track deep like a little railway-cutting, she must come—stern first. The anchor must be laid out astern as soon as we could float the dinghy. The anchor was therefore placed in the dinghy in readiness, with forty fathoms of chain; the exact position for the anchor was computed by alignment of objects on shore, and all was in readiness. The returning tide would creep up through greyness of the dawn; and, until then, we could do nothing more.

Robinson, with hands filthy from the chain, clambered back on board out of the dinghy. Though he still thirsted for action, he could not be accommodated. We could only linger in the low evening sunlight before turning in, and wait. Birds circled over the marshlands, and the tidal flats shimmered, reflecting the light.

"I'd hardly have believed it," he murmured. "Nothing could be duller, on the face of things, than squatting on the mud—just *left*. We can't get out and we can't get on. And yet, these flats give a sense—almost like the sea. Space, somehow, and mystery."

The sunlight grew richer, and then faded into gradual evening. Loth to turn in—despite the need for rising at about three in the morning, we were still on deck when dusk had fallen. The immense mud-flat was mysterious in twilight. There was never a sound unless some distant call of a bird from the marshland; we were alone.

The same tides brimmed over its face, bringing the cogs and carracks to ancient Woodbridge, and the same tides ebbed carrying them seaward again. Lawless and resolute, the old ship-masters sailed this Deben River; in ancient vessels, single-sailed, or in high-castled ships, with square headsails and lateen mizen, they came and went. Here as elsewhere, their weather-eye was always lifting for strange sails. Every other vessel was an object of suspicion; and—if truth be told—these ship-masters were themselves no better than they should be. Every one of them, though without conscious sense of it, was imbued deeply with Darwin's principle of the survival of the fittest. Only by swiftness, efficiency and strength could life and traffic be maintained. Great lords ashore, men of honour in their own day, knew the honour of the sword only, and were indifferent in matters of property saving their own. A man's claim to his belongings became flimsy when one stronger appeared. True, the law existed. But the law, on the seas and tidal fringes of the land, was remote and ineffectual; it curbed the piratical seaman no more than King Canute had curbed the waves.

So the Middle Ages, with their lawless figures of self-confident manhood, went by. And although Henry VII and VIII, our first kings who were really alive to the importance of maritime affairs, made great efforts towards protection and ordering of sea-borne trade, piracy was still rampant in the

RAMSHOLT CHURCH.

days of Elizabeth. John Flicke, of Woodbridge, was a "regular receiver" of pirates' booty, and was continually being fined. The traffic was perpetual. In 1579 five gentlemen of Woodbridge were ordered to appear before the Privy Council to answer an accusation that Arithway Newport, a notorious pirate, had escaped arrest through their connivance. Piracy—like smuggling of later years—was altogether too lucrative, and half the country-side was in league with the offenders.

But not in lawlessness only did the vigorous manhood of the age find expression. Men of Woodbridge were bearing a man's part in commerce and enterprise abroad. John Foxe, for instance, gunner of a Levant merchantman which was taken by the

Turks in 1563, was a Woodbridge man. A tough fellow of indomitable resource, he never lost courage during his slavery. Schemes of escape miscarried, but he persisted, dogged always. Finally, in 1577, after infinite pains, his hour arrived; at the head of 266 fellow-slaves he overpowered and killed the guards, and seized a galley—in which, with only eight casualties, the whole party escaped. Sun-parched and wasted, John Foxe returned to old Woodbridge town after fourteen years in slavery, and Queen Elizabeth granted him a pension of 1*s*. a day, "in consideration of the valiantnes done in Turkey."

Such were the figures that might haunt this twilight. Just such a flood-tide as would brim landward under to-morrow's dawn brought up the vessel of old John Foxe or of the grim shipmen long dead before the Middle Ages; their homes were upon the shores about us.

> "The day returns, but never more
> Returns the traveller to the shore,
> And the tide rises, the tide falls."

Robinson yawned, without stint or concealment.

"Time to turn in?" I queried.

"I suppose so," he admitted, "but one wants to see the whole clock round at this game; it's all so good that every hour is too good to miss."

It is just my own feeling, and for that reason, though after years, I am for ever filching just one more hour from sleep, for just one hour more of vigil in the night-silence of these haunted creeks and inlets.

Prosaically setting the alarm-clock, I turned in; and next moment, or so it seemed, the clock was whirring hideously. Unbelievably soon, grey dawn had broken, and I stretched and yawned, altogether reluctant.

But, once on deck, the old charm was re-asserted, for here—stealthily in the greyness—was that smooth tide brimming landward. Under a clouded sky it was unruffled—its surface smooth as oil. Thunder was booming somewhere in the background.

"I could have spared the thunder," I told Robinson as he joined me. "Suppose a wind-squall from it breaks at the critical moment, it may tip the scale against us."

As soon as the dinghy had stirred with the deepening flood, the anchor had been laid out, and the event would soon be declared. Either the yacht would remain stationary and pull the anchor towards her, or (as we trusted) the anchor would be staunch. The yacht would then be dragged—as the cable came in over the windlass—down from her perch on the mud and into the fairway.

It was high water. The slack of the chain was taken up on the winch, and the critical moment had arrived. Thunder boomed round the horizon, but no rain fell, and the water—under leaden cloud—was still mirror-like. The chain was taut and quivered, as the handle of the winch turned with its regular clank, clank, hauling it home. Clank, clank, clank, the chain came in. Clank, clank, clank

—what an endless amount of iron links there seemed to be, coming in slowly over the stern and dropping, in endless procession, into the hold after they passed

WALDRINGFIELD

over the winch. Clank, clank, clank, more still (was the anchor dragging after all?); clank, clank, clank, and no sign of a move. Clank, clank—yes, yes, we had shifted; easily now the chain came home—there was no drag of the keel through mud, she was afloat.

We anchored in the fairway, and let the tide drop from the flats before we made sail for the sea. That berth of ours upon the mud was soon laid bare by the ebbing water; the great gash cut by the yacht's keel, and the deep trough in it where her shape had settled—these were lettered with no uncertain hand. Some few tides would be needed

RAMSHOLT

to smooth those prints of ours from the Kingston mud.

A breeze freshened in the storm's wake. The thunder had gone. Past Waldringfield we sailed and its pleasant anchorage. The deep water—not there meandering midway in the expanse of mud—curves close inshore beside a little wooded cliff and a hard shore. A small bevy of boats is always at anchor, and landing can be effected at all states of the tide.

Below Waldringfield is a " horse " in mid-channel —" horse " being the name given to banks that crop up with rounded backs like the back of a horse. When covered by the tide, its position is shown clearly to the observant by the strong ripple upon it; and at low water it cannot be missed even by the most unobservant—for it dries out, and can be walked on.

Further seaward still is Ramsholt; wooded and rich, the banks are a picture. The old church tower is there, and mossy farmsteads—a haunt of ancient peace.

It was at Waldringfield that I gossiped about the river with a native, who summarised the position in a sentence. One quiet evening at sundown, the two of us were leaning against a rail, looking across the broad face of water. The tone of sunset pervaded everything, and silence was perfect. I had told him of more than one experience, and we were just parting.

He nodded his head at me and spoke like an oracle. " *Lots on 'em gets stuck wot's used to it, let alone strangers,*" was his parting word; and he turned landward, towards the sunset.

CHAPTER VII

THE TIDES OF ORFORD HAVEN

ORFORD HAVEN, in its bay of shingle, is really heart and centre of that Suffolk sea-border which once was great. The name becomes now little more than a survival, but

> "The very music of the name has gone
> Into my being."

It is a name that stands from of old, rounded and euphonious. It brings its own visions and its own mysteries.

We were bound for Orford Haven to-day. From the Essex coast we were beating northward. There had been a really strong blow from the north for a couple of days, but now the wind had fallen to a stiff breeze.

"These waves are more like the Channel than the North Sea," I was saying, "big deep rolling fellows like these. We don't often attain such dignity here."

The waves were the aftermath of yesterday's storm. And the weather was not too genial yet: the coast-line lay dark indigo, under clouds. Then a scurry of rain blotted it in patches. To north of us, cut with a knife, was the remote outline of Orfordness lighthouse.

"See the lighthouse, Robinson?" I asked him. ("I ain't blind," he said, but I took no notice.) "It comes up out of the sea. Detached. The coast it stands on is hull-down, so to speak. It's below the horizon."

Smudges of steamer-smoke lay to eastward, but the ships themselves were lost, hull-down also.

"Fores'l sheet is foul of something," Robinson said, as he lifted himself nimbly from the well, and slipped cat-like for'ard. "All clear, haul away," he called, balancing himself to the heave of the yacht as she lifted over the long wave and splashed into the trough. He lingered for a moment, and the salt sea-wind tossed the spray about him. His joy in the fact of sea and wind was infectious.

He was again beside me in the well. "Hollesley Bay?" he was saying, "yes, I remember."

Hollesley Bay it was—a noted anchorage in the days of sail. Extending from Orfordness to Orford Haven, inside the Whiting Shoal, the anchorage was 4 miles long and $1\frac{1}{2}$ miles wide; and, by shore or by shoal, it was protected from every quarter except N. to N.E.

Grenville Collins, surveying these waters in the reign of King Charles II, said that "Hoseley Bay is a very good place to Anchor, you having the Sands without, and is very good clean ground."

The anchorage, almost deserted now, has had

NELSON'S FLAGSHIP RETURNING FROM THE BALTIC, 1801

its long pages of history. Thus earlier generations at Orford Haven, like the old farmhouse of Fitzgerald's poem,

> "... once discerned the smoke
> Of old sea battles far away,
> Saw victorious Nelson's topmasts
> Anchoring in Hollesley Bay."

Nelson, upon his return from the Baltic in 1801, came home to an England greatly perturbed. Napoleon's threat of invasion was just then hanging like a nightmare, and the popular trepidation could be allayed by the appointment of one man and one man only. "The unreflecting multitude," as Southey wrote soon afterwards, "were not to be persuaded that an invasion could only be effected by numerous and powerful fleets. A general alarm was excited; and, in condescension to that unworthy feeling, Nelson was appointed to a command extending from Orfordness to Beachy Head, on both shores—a sort of service, he said, for which he felt no other ability than what might be found in his zeal."

Nelson had soon so acted that "he did not believe they could get three miles from their ports." But coastal defence was not neglected. Among other measures adopted was the anchoring of armed barges in the river at Orford Haven, and the Sea Fencibles were called out. This force, created in 1798, consisted of fishermen and boatmen and various types of longshoremen; it was recruited with comparative ease, because enrolment afforded protection against impressment for service with the main fleets at sea.

We had seen just a hint of the sterner aspect of this haven on our last entry, though there blew then only a capful of wind and no hurricane; and to-day, as we again approached it, I told Robinson of its iniquities.

There are times when the entry, for all the good offices of the pilot, can be odious enough. The *North Sea Pilot* has it thus:

"Should a vessel be forced to run for the haven when the pilots cannot venture off, they then station themselves upon the leading beacons and direct the course to be steered by the waving of flags."

Now, as I told Robinson, I know the look of that entrance at times, and I felt that a man with a flag would fail to console me. Racing straight for the

AFTER COPENHAGEN

surf-line until one's ears are well-nigh deaf with the roar of it, half-blind with the whipping spray or wholly blind in some sudden scurry of rain, that career haven-ward would rival any nightmare. The man with the flag would be lost in the rain-squall, and here would be the breakers and the shingle close aboard, every shore-mark gone. Such a case is extreme. But it is convincing. Not for me.

Robinson braced his foot against the bulkhead and hauled in the jib-sheet, for we had just gone about, standing off-shore again. The Martello towers of the low coast-line were passing, and the haven was in sight.

"If it were ever as bad as that," I continued, "I shouldn't attempt it. I should carry on, northward."

"Humber, or Scapa?" he queried, with that quick smile of his.

He knew that there was little chance of the pilot refusing to favour us on any day that I was likely to be hovering at the entry. With a south-westerly wind, strong even to the point of vice, the seas moderate wonderfully as one closes the shore. In some savage easterly wind the pilots might have the flags ready, but I fancy that only vessels in a bad case already would be running for Orford Haven *then*.

Nevertheless, I have heard of uncomfortable cases, and I recalled for Robinson's ear—as nearly as I could—the words of one grubby barge-master. Battered beyond the ordinary, and quite disreputable, he yet kept his barge in the acme of condition; and, from a seamed and wizened face, that eye of his was still bright to windward.

"If I'd a known that wind was a-comin' on me, I hadn't ought to a bin there," he had said. "No, I reckon I didn't," he repeated, reflectively. "That wind it come it over me, proper. My ole berge, she wanted pilotage; but that there pilot, he didn't want me, not just then. Blowed suthen wicked, that did. So that pilot feller, he up by them there beacons, he was a-wavin' *flegs*. Beggared I couldn't see him, not that way I couldn't—spray a-drivin'

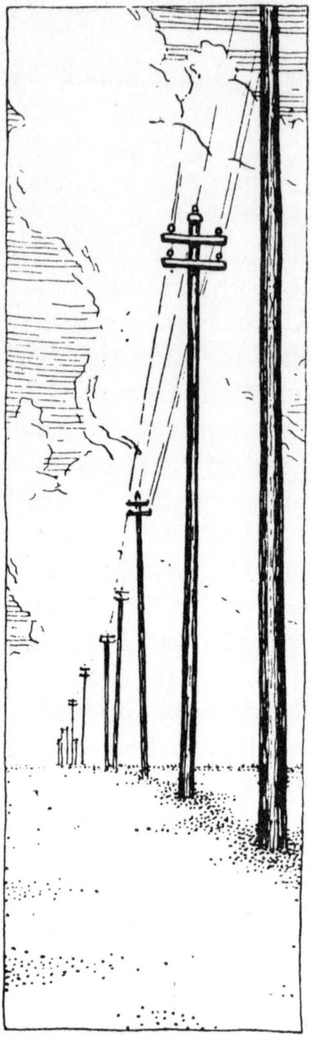

– SHINGLEBANK –

an' rain. Rum 'un if we hit that there little tide-way and get in, I thought to myself, and then wal-lopp we hit summat else. *Shingle? Pebbles?* They smothered the old berge. *Pebbles?* I'd got 'em in me eyes an' mouth, *got 'em in me pockets!* Me, I tumbled clean over, half-hit the wheel and went down whack, the moment she struck. An' I hopped up, I grabbed hold o' the wheel an' rubbed me eyes. Beggared we weren't *inside the bloomin' haven*, right inside, running up with the tide like a bloomin' escaped lunatic.

"Pilot, he come up after I anchored. 'We see you bounce on that knoll,' he says, 'an' we knew you'd come in right enough there,' he says. 'Couldn't do nothin' else, not if you tried. We knew that tide was boun' to fetch you right in; tide run, in this haven, like a sluice,' that's wot he says when he come up after I anchored."

There is not a doubt of it. The most compelling feature of the haven is its tide; the tide gives Orford Haven its character. Running at $7\frac{1}{2}$ knots, it exacts respect in proportion. Sailing vessels have no thoughts of entering against the ebb. Seen from the shore, there is little to indicate this decisive factor; but, afloat, it simply dominates.

Swinging ably over the long swell, the yacht beat on. At the South Whiting Buoy it was "lee-ho" for the last time. Pointed shoreward again, she would carry right away into the haven.

A schooner and barquentine were still at anchor close in to Orfordness, where they had evidently ridden out the storm. Our own bowsprit was pointed towards the Coastguard cottages, and she looked as if she must fetch Shinglestreet. Up went our pilot jack. In a few minutes we should be in the haven.

"Where's the wind gone?"

My voice was one of protest and even consternation, for the wind had left us. All in a single instant it had decamped; not a breath remained. We were powerless, at mercy of the tide.

Robinson tried to look sympathetic, but only succeeded in laughing. Inside the haven or outside, it was all one to him so long as he was afloat and free. It was I who wanted to make good my passage and to get inside. On the flood, the great body of water—the whole sea-face—moves solidly southward along the coast. Through Orford

Haven it doubles round at swifter pace and romps northward up the river. Here in the open it was sweeping full-tilt a-southward.

A-southward perforce we went with it, like any bit of flotsam, lifeless. Then, for a moment, a cat's-paw of wind ruffled the water, and she held her own; but it too faded, and she dropped sternwise again.

It was hard lines. For if only we'd managed to get close inshore, north of the haven, the tide could have done the rest. It would have sucked her in, swiftly and incontestably. But here the tide was no friend of ours.

The kedge-anchor was sent with a splash over the bows; the rope tautened and the sternway ceased abruptly.

"Bound to get a squall or something with a puff of wind," I said hopefully, as I scanned those ugly grey clouds. "There's wind up above."

The clouds were shouldering purposefully across the sky, but not a whisper of air moved on the sea.

"Here it comes." The remark was simultaneous.

A live breath fluttered, and Robinson's quick hands were busy on the dripping kedge-warp. We watched the objects on the shore-line. The church was slipping behind the Martello tower in the right direction; we were sailing. Yes . . . yes . . . but no, the church paused and hovered, then it began sliding the other way.

"No good. Let go."

Another draught came and another, and again and again the manœuvre was repeated. . . .

"There's a proper rain-squall coming," I said. "Look at it, a real right-down black squall."

With genuine approval I watched the inky cloud. We buttoned our oilskins up to our eyes; hand on tiller, I stood—poised, expectant.

"Ye little fishes, what rain!" My companion chuckled at the fantastic perpendicular fury of it, as the solid rainfall bounced and rebounded from the smooth sea and made rivers on the deck. "Quite refreshing, keep the deck-seams tight," he chirped, as he hunched his streaming shoulders from the deluge of it. Rain came like a waterfall, smothering us, but not a breath of wind.

The rain lessened; we could hear it drip-drip-dripping everywhere. Then it came again, whitening the water. But still the air was dead.

At long last, as the rain tailed off into a subdued patter, a vital touch quickened from eastward. This was the real thing; swiftly we gathered way and swept towards the haven. Then, before it had time to flatten, we had taken the pilot on board and the in-going current had us; almost out of control, we were swept, sent coursing like a cork in a rain-brimmed gutter round the sharp bend. Answering her helm in another draught of wind, the yacht was sailing in the river. She was inside the haven.

Dependent wholly upon natural harbourage, the commerce of the Middle Ages resorted to many tidal rivers which, insignificant to modern shipping, were ample then. Orford, with its high castle, was a thriving town; it built ships in its shipyards and it traded with the Continent. The haven was probably then nearer the town, for the shoaling of the river has carried the entrance southward; but in all essentials it must stand almost recognisably the same. Broad-beamed and sturdy, the carracks came and went, and they were no great vessels then which despised havens guarded by a shallow bar. They entered thankfully, safe from the sea. The word haven, a "place of safety for ships," is of ancient Dutch origin, and the old-world Dutch and Flemish ship-masters let go their anchors here. With pleasant unconcern they heard the sea batter on the pebbles outside as the storm darkened. Or, in lighter winds that followed, they set their broad sails and swung out seaward with the ebb. Such in its own time, a port that stirred with modern commerce, was Orford Haven.

It has had its day; its life has been lived. The ancient name holds its haunting savour, but the haven has become—between those stretches of bare shingle-bank—a deserted waterway.

A flat shore of barren shingle, remote from towns and railways, the place lies unwanted and undiscovered. Few reach it from the shoreward side. Barges and yachts, bound for Aldeburgh, may enter and pass; they are few and solitary. Otherwise there are only the gulls that circle, and the weather-beaten pilots who, lingering beside some boat hauled up on the shingle, scan the far-away ships that pass on the sea-line.

Yarns in plenty there are of the haven and its

THEIR TARRY BOATS UPON A PEBBLY BEACH

bar and its tide. If ever ignored, the tide is apt to exact notice with uncomfortable vigour.

"Don't anchor too far down," said a boatman to me when I told him that I should be dropping down from Aldeburgh one day and anchoring just above the haven. "Ships get swept out by the ebb; tide run like a horse; ships get swept right out, and only bring up when the waves breakin' throw 'em on the shingle heaps outside. Get off then? No. There ain't no anchor ever made I've heard could do that job. Tell you for why. The anchor, it just runs through the loose shingle, same's through water, and never tries to bite.

"As I'm tellin' you," he went on, "a smart little craft, she got carried out and thrown on one of those knolls. Surf outside didn't take long about it either. Sea a-showin' his ivory, proper. Broke up *in one tide*, broke clean up, that's what *that* little craft did."

The way (it may be explained) in which a ship thrown ashore but as yet undamaged will ordinarily extricate herself is this. She will lay out an anchor into deep water from a boat. If, when the cable is hauled in on the ship, the anchor holds fast in the ground, the ship is pulled out towards the anchor the whole time at exactly the same pace as the cable comes on board; if, on the other hand, the anchor does *not* hold fast, the anchor comes home as the chain is hauled in, and the ship remains where she was. The loose shingle at Orford Haven gives no hold, and so the anchor comes home every time, and the ship is at the mercy of the waves.

"Yes, I allow it's a funny place for them what don't know," a fisherman repeated. "Runs seven knots an' more over all that loose shingle, and the whole place is movin'. *You can hear the whole bottom runnin' along with it*, tide a-suckin' an' racin', an' all the shingle runnin' with the run of it."

The story of the Coastguards' boat is one of the tragedies of the place. "Always unhandy in a boat," the fishermen, of course, will tell you. The

Coastguards had been to Aldeburgh and were perhaps less staid than usual. Returning to Shingle-street, they had no intention of leaving the river.

BEACH BOATS

But the mad tide swept them out, and all eight of them save one were drowned. Some of the bodies were recovered near by, but one of them had been carried by the returning flood-tide right up to Orford before it was found, while another was swept out seaward and was ultimately picked up in the *Thames*.

The fishermen of Aldeburgh and Orford pilot their own boats in and out.

" Time back, we gotter bring an ole yacht up from Burnham," a fisherman told me, " jes' me an' my mate, no one else on board. We come away in weather a little dirty, but wind fair. We pulled down two reefs, wind a-backin' sou'-easterly and weather not lookin' up to much. Then we come through it like smoke. 'She'll sail herself right under, this way,' I shouted to my mate, 'we'll pull down that there third reef,' an' so we did, but there weren't no stoppin' of her. Come like a train."

He paused and looked at me complacently. "Sea was roarin' all along the shingle, and pilots—as they tell me after—they sight us standin' straight in. Didn't reconnise us, boat bein' strange. 'Nothin' can't save her,' one says to the other, seein' us a-roarin' in same's that, full afore the wind. Sea, as I tell you, was all one great tumble o' white foam all along the bar. Thought we was doomed, *they* did," he added with relish. "'Nothin' can't save her; doomed she is,' they says.

"Then they see'd us shape course, same 's they would themselves. 'She's comin' in,' they says, 'there's some bloke wot knows somethin' aboard of her, after all.' Quite excited-like, they come runnin' down, wonderin'. We see 'em.

"Man an' boy, I've crossed that bar more times 'n I care to count," he continued. "Been out when I wished I hadn't, and yet come home all right. But I never crossed the bar worser'n that. Up that little yacht come on a great wave, and then the wave sput her in, *threw* her same 's a young 'un might toss a ball. If she went true, in she comes. If she didn't, if she hit that there shingle, not much

ONE OF NELSON'S FRIGATES

wouldn't interest us after that. Not *this* side," he added grimly, " I reckon."

I gathered from his account that the boat had negotiated the passage, triumphant. When, however, I mentioned the incident to one of the pilots some time afterwards, he broke in upon my story, quiet but decisive. " Tidy mess they'd 'a bin in, too, if we hadn't bin standin' by," he said darkly. The ground being controversial, I probed no further, and can only place the two statements side by side.

" Well, that's that," said Robinson, peeling an apple which he had mysteriously purloined from somewhere below. " As a seaport, I call it elementary. There's no harbour, no shipping, and plenty of chances of getting broken up. But," and he looked back along the range of shingle to the broken entrance, " there's a strangeness and mystery about it, a sort of echo. It once was."

And he was right: that is Orford Haven. With its ancient record of stirring business and rich merchandise, it is now but a silent haven, with yarns only of longshoremen and little boats. The world has withdrawn and left it. There remain only the yellow shingle-banks, with the sea-gulls that wheel and settle about the tide-washed knolls.

CHAPTER VIII

ALDEBURGH AND ITS TIDAL SHALLOWS

BUMP of a boat alongside dispelled our drowsiness. Morning had dawned hours ago, but without virtue or inducement, for rain stampeded over the decks, and the only sound beside was a tumult of wind and water. Wash-wash-wash, the fretful waves outside were thrashing on the yacht, intimately heard through the walls that separated us—in such close neighbourhood; and the yacht was rocking to them, rocking.

The rain had swept above us all night; and all night long the whine and patter and splash had been a lullaby. Secure in the river off Aldeburgh, we had been indifferent; the elements were welcome to their spurt of ill-temper. We had even slept the better for the noise of it. Then, on lazily awakening, we had drowsed off once more, half-conscious—hearing the swept rain with its swift touches innumerable, and the wind.

The bump of that boat awakened us; it was the shipwright, come to effect some small repair. We caught one glimpse of a sturdy figure, in oilskins and sou'-wester that streamed with rain, as he came aboard.

" Better down there below than this—it ain't

much class outside, I reckon." He grumbled with an entire cheerfulness as he tossed his tools aboard, and made fast the boat's painter. "I'd stay down in the dry if I was you."

This idle interlude, with no tyrannical tide to gainsay our leisure, was as unusual as it was welcome. The boots of that good fellow overhead sounded heavily, as noises will upon a yacht, and then the hammer-hammer-hammer commenced.

"I told him to be early," I explained to Robinson, "so that we shouldn't miss the tide at twelve. But he's a sturdy Briton to be punctual on a morning like this."

"A time for everything," Robinson murmured from the bunk opposite, "a time to work and . . . a time to be idle." And he pulled the blankets up to his chin again.

ALDEBURGH

THE · MOOT · HALL · ALDEBURGH

But, before long, the hammering was too much for us, and we turned out of our bunks.

"Thank God for my good breakfast and a lid to cover us," said Robinson half an hour later, as the rain swept in a vicious little hurricane overhead.

. . . . . .

We went ashore in the dinghy. The heavier drench of rain was subsiding, but rain still spattered and dripped, and the distances were settled grey.

"Come this way again?"

A boatman greeted me as I secured the dinghy. "Last time you come you anchored in the bay outside."

His was a good memory, for it had been two years ago. "That rain'd summat last night," he added with

SHIP BUILT AT ALDEBURGH, 17TH CENTURY. (AT FOOT: COMMON SEAL OF ALDEBURGH)

a chuckle. "Don't want no deck-caulkin' gone amiss, *them* little showers."

Rain or no rain, Aldeburgh had its old charm as we paced along the sea-front. But the shoreward waves are grim companions, when one remembers how much they have levelled that was once firm and orderly; and they still threaten. In a map dating from the first year of the reign of Queen Elizabeth (1559), there are shown to be denes, or flats, between Aldeburgh and the sea. Aldeburgh was a "place of considerable magnitude," and the church was ten times more distant from the shore than now. The Moot Hall, now at front of the town, was then at the back. There were shops and cobbled streets, and houses with casements lamplit in the evenings, where the waves are now breaking. The sea has devoured them.

"MARYGOLD," CONTRIBUTED BY ALDEBURGH TO THE FLEET OF DEFENCE AGAINST THE ARMADA, 1588

Contrasting Aldeburgh with the river-ports of Orford and Woodbridge, old Robert Reyce said (in 1618) that " Aldborough is full vppon the maine sea." The position has brought its own penalties.

We were soon back on board, and were getting a reef tied up in the mainsail. Robinson, as usual, was in a passion of energy to get under way. Merely for the sake of keeping him happy, we were to sail southward a little before turning in serious earnest to explore up-river. Our white sails looked grey in the murky air; grey too were land and water. It was not cheerful outwardly, but we were cheery enough, the two of us together.

" Shipbuilding—*here?*" Robinson questioned sceptically. " Extraordinary how everything's gone."

Yet Aldeburgh built great ships on its own slipways in the reigns of Elizabeth and James I. *Marygold* was the town's contribution to the fleet fighting the Armada. And from generation to generation the prosperous shipyard work continued, until, in 1650, Henry Johnson of Aldeburgh (a descendant of Francis Johnson who had commanded the *Marygold*) opened the Blackwall Yard near London. Then it was that shipyard work gradually left Suffolk in favour of the Thames.

Robinson had taken the helm, and the yacht was reaching over the tide—the shingle-bank beside her.

" It's an almighty matter-of-fact morning," he said, as he turned up the collar of his oilskin again,

A SHIP OF KING CHARLES II, CALLING TO PROVISION AT ALDEBURGH

" but you don't need to tell me that there were smugglers here. The place was made for them; I can almost fancy I see them busy."

Smuggling, I might have told him, was conducted

on such a scale that, in 1720, six vessels ran cargoes in a single night, and there were *three hundred men* along the shore to receive the run. The Preventive officers had been cowed—or bought.

Long before that the Aldeburgh of Elizabethan days had thriven upon piracy. The Aldeburgh burgesses themselves were fined for having profited by it. In 1579 the town was searched on the Queen's authority, and pirates' plunder was everywhere discovered. Martin Frobisher was, on another occasion, arrested on account of a prize he brought into Aldeburgh, and was sent to the Marshalsea Prison. But he contrived to escape without serious punishment.

Later on the boot was on the other leg. The town suffered heavily from Dunkirk privateers (those "Silly Dunkirkes," as Reyce called them). Then, in 1656, there was war with Spain, and a naval lieutenant—in search of men—came ashore with a press-gang. He appears to have suffered. He reported that he was abused by the bailiffs and constables and stoned by the people, who routed his men.

Ten years later (2nd July, 1666) a Dutch Fleet, eighty strong, was sighted. The town was in a ferment, for a landing appeared imminent; then, with relief after a period of pulsing uncertainty, the townsmen watched the fleet sail southward. In actual fact it shaped course towards Harwich and attacked Landguard Fort.

Next we hear of a King's ship, a year or two later, calling to provision at Aldeburgh; and so low was

"THE · SAME · SLOOPS · STICKING · SIDELONG · IN THE · MUD · AS · SIXTY · YEARS · AGO."

the credit of King Charles's Government that the captain had to leave six barrels of gunpowder as security for payment before they would hand over a thing to him.

During those years Aldeburgh was a busy port, and there were twenty hoys to and from London every week. Defoe says that, as a seaport, Aldeburgh "throve upon the decay of Orford"; but both are of little enough account now.

"It's an oddity, this river," Robinson was saying. "If you go up the mast, you see the waves breaking just beyond the shingle-bank, but it's twenty miles to reach that shore by water."

AN ALDEBURGH HOY, EIGHTEENTH CENTURY

It is a fact. The course of the river Alde, eccentric beyond the ordinary, lends its own touch of strangeness to the town of Aldeburgh. Heading merrily in a bee-line direct for freedom and the open sea, it is discouraged by the merest of shingle-banks. The shingle is only a few dozen yards wide, but off goes the intimidated river, hounding away southward to find a way out. With its sluicing ebb, it has romped and twisted ten miles or so, often within hail of the sea, before it succeeds in escaping.

Edward Fitzgerald, coming to Aldeburgh in the 'eighties, found the "same sloops sticking sidelong in the mud as sixty years ago." And he would probably find it little altered still. Slaughden Quay is no work of modern science. The grey water-worn piles must be little different from those of the wharf upon which the poet Crabbe worked as a day-labourer, piling up butter-casks, before he went off in the sloop *Unity* to London to make his fortune. And when the tide is out, there are the boats still found to complete the picture by "sticking sidelong in the mud," with masts that heel awry, this way and that.

Above Aldeburgh is a large tidal lake. At low water the expanse of tidal flat is out, and just one desultory trickle of deep water wanders through it. Then, as the tide rises, it is one broad lake again; but the tide over the flats is shallow, and the wandering channel—now lost and undeclared—must be faithfully followed, or the ship will be caught by the shallows, and—there remain.

"Woodbridge over again?" Robinson chuckled.

"Only worse," I told him, and he turned expectantly, for he scented misfortunes.

"On one board" (I was speaking of a couple of years earlier) "the yacht had carried a foot or so too far, and . . . she was on. *That* didn't worry anyone, for the tide was rising. It was just a case of laying out the kedge. But time after time the kedge pulled home through that black sludge, cutting through it like a knife through butter in the dog-days."

"Keep your hands clean?" he chuckled, remembering his own experiences.

"I've never met such noisome filth. It's . . . well, never mind that. I got plastered properly before I'd done. I tried the big anchor—no use. And, as the tide rose, she edged and sagged further and further over the flats. It was a hard wind, or one might have been able to tow her. . . ."

"So that it meant a night-berth, like at Woodbridge?"

"No. Just at top of the tide, by rare good fortune, she decided to come off under sail. But it's a foul hole, once you're out of the channel."

LAYING OUT THE KEDGE

Since then I had again been up, this time to Snape Bridge, and in someone else's yacht. Impressed by the tortuousness of the fairway and the economy of beacons, I proposed to-day to ship an Aldeburgh boatman as pilot. Back to Aldeburgh we sailed and took him on board.

That sturdy wind which had been roaring from the due west had abated, but our two reefs were still needed, and we heeled away with long white slashes of broken water to either side of us, as we whirled to and fro, beating through the fleet of anchored yachts.

" Nice shape she is—cod's head and a mackerel's tail, as the Cornishmen says," the boatman observed, as he watched her. "Very handy, yes, I see she is."

The hard breeze suited her. After scattering the foam about, and giving the Aldeburgh yachts a roll on her wash, she became more staid on the longer boards, but not less vigorous. Her vigour only slackened when the wind fell lighter, which it suddenly did; it fell to a whole-sail breeze, and the reefs were shaken out.

" One tall tree in a hedge—yes, lower on the slope, that's what us chaps go by. That stay in line with the dark tree yonder."

On the green hillside and landscape to which he pointed there were hedges many, and tall trees and dark trees in plenty. These leading-marks were not of the simplest.

So wide and honest did the broad face of water look, wind-furrowed as it lay there, that it gave no hint of shallowness. It was leaden-grey under the clouds. A few birds in the distances grouped and scattered. Otherwise we were utterly alone.

" 'Course I know it well." The boatman was again speaking. " 'Long here with the punt and the gun in winter. Up those shores, you don't want to leave the punt too long; tide, that tide run off the flat all in a moment, in a manner of speakin'. Yes, I'd let her come now, sir."

" IN THE VERY HEART OF THE COUNTRY "

Curlews round the margins again rose and settled, and a few distant herons stood solitary. " Frank " is the old Suffolk name for heron. And it used to be said that each curlew "carried a shilling on its back," that being its market price. The wind rifted the clouds and brought a slant of sunlight. Stray colour drifted over the landscape.

"Soft mud you say, sir? Kedge won't hold in it? I allow it often won't. Us chaps drive a spar hard into it and haul on that. Better hold that way."

So we beat to and fro, making inland.

" Hullo," and he gave a soft whistle, for she had missed stays. She was on.

" That spit, the

FROM IKEN CLIFF

other side the Mansion Crik, I doubt it isn't shoaling outward," he reflected ruefully. The yacht lay over, inert, with sails drawing. "Never mind, happen she'll soon blow over it." The main obstruction lay to weather of her, and so she did.

Up the twistings beside Iken Church, where the channel at one spot positively doubles back, and well-nigh ties itself into a loop, the boatman took the helm; thus we reached the tree-covered slope of Iken cliff, and dropped our anchor in deep water, preposterously close inshore. There is a sandy beach, and the whole place is a very perfect little haven—if a trifle inaccessible. Folded among the greenery, with the singing of birds about us, there was a softness and luxury about it all, after the barrenness of shingle-banks and the wind-scoured sea outside.

We deferred return until the banks were just beginning to uncover, or at least to declare their position by the appearance of the water. We had wandered ashore over the down-side, and along farm tracks in the very heart of the country. A farm-hand sitting side-saddle on one great cart-horse while he led another passed us in a country lane—quite a picture. And now we were back on board, and the yacht was again away, bound seaward.

For the present we were at one with the peace of the landscape. The breeze was falling lighter still and evening was upon us.

Quietly in the dusk we slid over the flat calm water, following the knots of the tortuous little fairway. Even when the flats, by beginning to

SNAPE BRIDGE

uncover, showed the course of the channel, one was glad to have the local expert. Things were not too self-evident in the failing light.

"What, again?"

The words, if spoken, were not aloud. The local boatman had been at the helm, but he sprang now to seize the quant-pole. With our united efforts we succeeded in disengaging her from the mud-bank.

"Ain't really got steerage way," he apologised. "That wind, it's all died away in here. Trees an' all, they close it off." Obviously he was a little mortified.

When a yacht has no real way on her, it is not an easy matter to twist her successfully round the one or two elbow bends of this narrow channel.

He took one of the long sweeps which the yacht carried, and worked away with it, in order to keep her going a little faster than the tide. She was thus under control, although the wind had gone, and the great mere opening ahead of us was like one vast polished mirror.

" Swipes are useful," he said appreciatively, as he shipped the sweep again. We were now in wider water, and the fairway was less exacting. " All fallen to a smolt," he added—an old Suffolk equivalent for dead calm.

The time was one when dreams might be abroad in the twilight. Robinson was silent, and so was I.

> " Rest after toil, port after stormy seas,
> Ease after war, death after life, do greatly please."

And Snape Common, close at hand, was no unfitting place for the ship-burial of the Viking Northman. The old ship-master and ship warrior took his rest here for ten centuries undisturbed before the spade laid bare the ribs of his long-ship. Between the heaths and forests of virgin England the stern-faced rowers had brought him on his last voyage; unbuffeted here by the cold seaways, the long keel slid over the lake and past the brow of Iken cliff—" rest after toil, port after stormy seas."

Long before that, when the woaded Britons were still hunters in the forest, a lonely outpost of Roman civilisation had been established somewhere on the Alde; with the same sunsets and the same tides. Little indeed, as seen in this gathering twilight, can

"IN THE LATE TWILIGHT, WE GLIDED WITH THE EBB"

AT IKEN CLIFF

have changed in the general aspect of the countryside.

And there was Snape Priory too, founded in Norman times. It, with the shadowy forms that once haunted its cloisters, has gone. In twilight of centuries it is lost.

Though to all seeming the wind was dead this evening, there was still a small breath to move the yacht. She was out now on the open mere. The airs, faint as they were, never blurred the perfection of the water-mirror with one smallest ripple. Bubbles and little waifs of floating weed moved unswervingly seaward with the silent seaward ebb, and the yacht (reflected in perfect image) slid gravely seaward with them. But—silent as she seemed—her way was to more purpose than that of the flotsam. Her canvas drooped lazily, but she faintly moved still—she was sailing.

Some bird in flight dipped to the water and rose again; a wide circle of tiny ripples spread and disappeared. A few birds were noisy for a moment on the wooded bank, they rose in a little bevy and vanished, and the sound was gone. Silence again was unruffled.

We hardly spoke, for it would have seemed like speaking aloud in a cathedral. A voice raised beyond a whisper would have been a violation, an outrage. Behind us was a wan flush of sunset in a sky grey otherwise, and ahead of us was a vague greyness of gathering night. Ghost-like in the late twilight we glided with the ebb.

CHAPTER IX

DRIFTING IN THE DARK TO ORFORD

IT was night. Night had that dead quality which is felt only when calm is stagnant and night-clouds have blotted the starshine. Silence was almost oppressive.

Off Slaughden Quay the yacht was technically under way; in bare fact she was drifting. Dark objects glimmered vaguely around her as she swam noiselessly through the anchorage.

"It's a weird passage," Robinson breathed; and he spoke in a whisper, just as if afraid of disturbing someone asleep.

In last twilight, at point of nightfall, there had still been some ghost of movement in the air, and one of those age-old specifics which smacksmen use would have betrayed the direction of it.

"Wet y'r finger in y'r mouth an' hold it up. Feels cold on the side the wind's a-comin' from."

The genteel alternative of wetting the finger overside in the water will not do. You must lick it honestly, every side of it. The *warm* moisture it is which is sensitive to any cool air that moves.

But now the night was windless. We carried no steering way, and we watched with some anxiety the anchored vessels that loomed through the darkness as we sidled helplessly through them on the ebbing water. Apart from the strong drift of tide, we should have been stock-still; as the smacksman might have said, "You wouldn't move a nutshell in an hour."

Dark enough in all conscience, the night was yet warm about us, and in that respect we differed comfortably from the oyster-dredgerman of Crabbe's poem:

> "He, cold and wet, and driving with the tide,
> Beats his weak arms against his tarry side,
> Then drains the remnant of diluted gin
> To aid the warmth that languishes within."

We were warm enough, and had no title at all to the gin prescription, but we were hungry. Beyond denial we were; it was half-past ten and we were dinnerless.

"Shall I get something, some bread and cheese?" Robinson was asking.

"No, we'll do better than that," I had answered. "We don't want to squander a bit of the ebb, but—we'll manage. We'll cook a proper dinner."

The sails, useless for the present, were furled. We were through the fleet of anchored vessels and were on clear water. So long as the wind remained dormant, the yacht would be slid along with all the flotsam of driftwood and seaweed, mid-channel—as she now was. Without pause she would drift seaward on the ebb. The night, through all the breadth of it, had not one breath of life, nor was there one least echo of a sound. Islanded in the night, in a mystery of gloom and dark water, we

"WHEN THE LIGHT SHINES STRAIGHT DOWN THE REACH"

left the yacht to her own devices. Helm and watch were forsaken; we both went below.

"Odd—to feel that she is loose and adrift," Robinson commented, as he put the cloth on and set the knives and forks. I was at the stove.

Unsteered, the old yacht would make several miles seaward, while our plates clattered and our glasses clinked in the bright cabin. She was blindly making good her way towards Orford. Several times, it is true, I thrust out my head from the genial lamplight into the dour reserve of darkness, just to make sure that she was still pursuing the same soundless way; for even a faint breath of beam-wind, catching her freeboard, would edge her gradually towards the water-smoothed mud. There would be no faintest sound, no sense of check, but she would just stop—unheard and unfelt. The tide would flow on seaward without her, and there she would remain, stranded till the returning flood should come up to refloat her.

But not a whisper disturbed the inexorable silence, not a breath. Without disturbance, we—in the lamplight below—had cooked and consumed our intended meal, and we were again on deck.

Along these reaches, often at night, the Aldeburgh boatmen still dredge and trawl, as they dredged and trawled in Crabbe's day. "Trole down there, night-time, we do," as one of them had said to me, a day or two back, "an' comin' up from Orford, when the light shines straight down the reach, then you know you're half-way home. 'Least" (he had added with sudden deprecation) "that's what us chaps say."

The recurrent beam from Orfordness lighthouse is visible, at its regular return of light after darkness, all the way. It had been our sole companion, a piece of clean-cut reality in a world of shadows. Seaward it is visible for fifteen miles. A lighthouse tower has stood on the shingle-bank since 1792; and for some centuries previously the light and seamark were located at Orford: there was then a beacon-light on Orford Castle. Somewhere in the darkness to southward of us, the ancient town of Orford was asleep in darkness, and its solid Castle keep towered above. Built in 1154, the grim keep had no eye to the convenience and safety of mariners, the whole breed of whom were broadly ignored by the landed lords; their thoughts turned landward, for science of the sea was as yet a pursuit not fitting. None the less, the rugged old mariners were at liberty to find the new Castle useful: kept in line with this object or that, it would ensure deep water for them. It became a recognised seamark for succeeding generations; through the Middle Ages the old lore was passed by word of mouth. Then Sailing Directions began to be written, and the mariner was told to "bring Orford Castle open of Balsey Cliff a sail's breadth"; for "the Castle and Church are high and may be seen six and seven leagues off, clear weather." The Castle was a signal station in the Napoleonic wars, and it is still used as a seamark for clearing Aldeburgh Napes; the church tower also (which is as old as the Castle) is used for clearing the Whiting Shoal.

ORFORD CASTLE

We let the yacht drift. The tidal mud was

uncovered on both sides of the fairway, but—being wet and glazed—it was indistinguishable from the water itself. The banks were a darker blot above the grey blur of the river. It was a strange scene.

"Dead-dark, and quiet as the tomb, it's almost creepy," my companion whispered in that same hushed key.

Midnight was past, and the clock's hand had touched the hour of one. The ebb-tide had little margin of life, it had weakened now, faltering towards slack-water. Our drift-time was over. One of us shuffled forward along the dark deck, and threw off the lashing from the anchor. Overboard with a splash went the hook, and the chain was paid, clattering, after it. We were anchored.

Then, as we peered through the darkness, wondering how far the friendly tide had carried us towards Orford, an object perched on the near sky-line caught my eye. A notice-board?

"Just our luck if it marks cables laid across under the water. Already our anchor may be foul of something," I grumbled. But I finished with a yawn. It would be time enough to examine things by daylight; we were both yawning now, and this world of shadows was a place for sleep. We went below.

Anxiety—as it proved—had been causeless; at 8.30 in the same morning, at the exact turn of the tide, the chain was shortened and the anchor came up at a touch. A grey world was about us. The flood-tide had swelled smoothly up the river while we slept, and all the shallows and low banks had been brimmed. It was high-water now; and we were away.

Things were blurred and low in tone; there was a sense of mist about the distances, but a light wind was abroad in this soft world, heading us. Without any crispness of decision, but with a slow certainty, the yacht beat seaward. The tide, rather than the wind, was again her friend; Orford lay visible to southward, darker grey in the wide grey glimmer of landscape; gradually its outline became firmer, and hardened into real solidity.

Orfordness lighthouse, solitary, stood now abeam.

"They're always so precise and tidy in a lighthouse," said Robinson. "They always put a night-cap over the lantern in the day, to keep the dust off."

But it is not of the dust that they are thinking; it is the sun. The lenses and prisms that multiply and concentrate the beam from the lamp are capable of concentrating such a beam of sunlight on the lamp that it would be melted to an utter ruin at once.

The yacht turned landward beside the King's Marshes to Orford. Between anchored boats her course twisted and doubled; then, just below the crumbling wharf and jetty, she let go her anchor.

Bound seaward on the present ebb, we must not be long, but a flying visit ashore could not be denied. The dinghy was made fast beside the steps; and the two of us were among the cottages of the old straggling township.

" Whatever it once was, it's a pearl of an old-world village now," Robinson commented, " and it's full of roses."

It is an inaccessible little corner, clean out of the world. The railway is miles away, and Aldeburgh is cut off from it by the river. It is thus quite isolated. Left high and dry, it has almost dwindled away. Even the Castle itself would have been levelled if the Government had not stepped in. Some earl who owned it was in act of pulling it down. But it was a known seamark, and the Government said No.

Strange it is to think, as one stands there, of its former greatness. Westward of the present town, those little country lanes—with their green hedges—still intersect on the same lines as did the cobbled town-alleys; they still bear the very names. The names of the old streets which echoed to the footfalls of burgess and shipman in the Middle Ages survive; the names remain, and nothing beside. Where houses were, there are meadows and trees, and wild-roses blossom in the hedgerows.

" It *is* remarkable," Robinson was saying, as he swung along the grass edges with his athletic stride. We paused on the turf beside the Castle keep. " Imagine," he said, " roofs clustered from here to the river, and any number of masts beside old-fashioned wharves. British coasters and Flemish carracks, eh? Well, it's empty enough now."

This was a still morning, and I think that we both felt a certain emptiness and silence in the whole region:

·THE·MARKET·PLACE AT ORFORD·

"Where over the grave of a city
The ghost of it stands."

Dunwich has become a grave and a memory because the sea roared in upon it, drowned it, and made it a ruin. But Orford was not destroyed. The site of Orford remains, and the ghost of its former self must somehow haunt these meadows.

They were not petty vessels of local trade only—those ships in the river. They were ships second to none in the harbours of the kingdom. The ships of the Plantagenets anchored in the fairway or warped up alongside the quays. Grim capable shipmen, the men in coarse falding, who were

Flemish Carrack setting sail from Orford Town:

grouped on the wharf or were noisy in the waterside taverns—these men were the ablest shipmen of their day. And they were a rough and lawless breed. Never safe on the high seas from the reckless pirates of the Middle Ages, they were equally ready to fight or—if occasion offered—themselves to turn picaroon. Thus in the year 1309 a peaceful merchantman from Bruges—lying at Orford — was attacked by a local bevy of pirates; the cargo was rifled and the vessel sunk.

A glance at the map will show that, just below Orford, the river at the present day takes a turn at right angles, and then heads directly seaward—as at Aldeburgh. As at Aldeburgh, it again suffers itself at the present day to be deflected, and does not reach the sea. But, as at Aldeburgh also, it once emptied itself at this point.

Just above Havergate Island is believed to have been the river-mouth at the time of Orford's greatness. In the days of Queen Elizabeth the shipyards were busy; and the town still prospered. But then gradually it declined. Defoe, in 1722, recorded this explanation:

" Orford was once a good town, but is decayed, and as it stands on the land side of the river the sea daily throws up more land to it, and falls off itself from it, as if it was resolved to disown the place and that it should be a seaport no longer."

Similarly we read in *The Suffolk Traveller* of a century later:

" The decline of the town is ascribed to the loss of its harbour, from the retiring of the sea, and a dangerous bar thrown up at its mouth by that overwhelming element."

There was a proposal in 1813 to cut a canal through to the sea and form the harbour anew. But the plan did not materialise, and the port has perished.

We were still standing at that great Castle mound, and I could see that Robinson was hugely impressed. He was grave and silent. He stood like a man abashed. This immense mound was artificially thrown up, and the walls were twenty feet thick. Like all Norman strongholds, the keep had its own well. Towering within circle of its moat and fortified bailey, the keep was self-contained. And it held the country-side in awe.

In 1215, Hubert de Burgh was lord of the Castle. In 1272, Hugh de Dennington, a robber-baron, was its master. Lawless marauders from the Castle spread terror landward; armed bands preyed as they would. Captives, as well as other spoil of robbery, went over the drawbridge, and the portcullis clanged behind. And the robbers were answerable to no man.

Then, in the reign of Edward I, William of Butley was lawlessly thrown into the dungeon. In sodden vaults, below level of the moat, he was chained, beyond rescue or pity. An ancient grudge was wiped out with grimmest cruelty; in the dungeons of Orford Castle, he was scourged to death, and his body secretly carried to sea and buried. These grim stones have their own history.

Our dinghy at the deserted little wharf was much lower than when we had left it—a reminder that the tide was falling fast. In a few moments we were on the yacht's deck, making sail.

It was a slow turn to windward, and we doubted whether we could contrive an escape to sea. If once the water were too low for us on the bar, we might reconcile ourselves to a quiet interlude. The level on the bar would soon again improve, but—against a racing flood-tide—exit would be hopeless. The tide would sweep us back in derision; we should have to wait for the next ebb.

But, under the grey skies with their hint of coming sunshine, misty as yet, we were not inclined to be fretful. The unbounded landscape was about us, and its sense of space was curiously great. Some

ANCHORED IN THE RIVER ORE.

poet there was, who, accustomed to fenlands, confessed himself uncomfortable among mountainous prospects. The mountains oppressed him; they were walls and barriers; they impeded the freedom of unimpaired distance. The long low sky-line was his choice.

Here we had full virtue of the low landscape. The haze enhanced its distance and its mystery. Our life was lived in the open.

The wind was freer as we passed Havergate Island; and, with the ebb under us, we were forereaching rapidly seaward. Here was the former river-mouth; and, on our starboard hand, would soon be the opening of Butley River, which takes its name from the old town and the Augustinian priory founded in 1171 by Ralph de Glanville.

On our port hand, as we slipped seaward, was the long line of shingle-bank again, with its chain of slender telegraph posts lessening into distance in each direction. The shore was utterly isolated as always.

Many wrecks have blown ashore upon its seaward side, but there is little record of them in local annals. They disappeared. Technically the Lord High Admiral had his rights in wrecks, and manorial rights were also recognised by law. Some of these rights were leased to the burgesses of the coast-towns; but the populace alongshore were always first upon the spot, and possession was nine points of the law. The prowling shore-folk made away with their plunder, and even destroyed the very ship also. Everything had disappeared before

ELIZABETHAN SHIP BUILT AT ORFORD
(AT FOOT: ARMS OF ORFORD)

slow-footed authority had arrived upon the scene.

But the smugglers, haunting these waters in later years, were less secret. In 1778 an armed gang of them ran a huge cargo in full light of day at Orford. Six revenue officers were present, but they were powerless in the face of numbers; they could do nothing but stand by and watch the roped barrels being piled in the farm carts of the shore-gang. In 1783 the contending forces were less unequal. A smuggling cutter drove ashore near Orford, and the revenue officers attacked. Beaten off at first, they obtained reinforcements of King's men, and—after a fierce struggle with cutlass and handspike—the cargo was captured. But the smugglers were not so easily denied. At dead of night they smashed their way into the revenue storehouse and carried off the whole consignment.

As the yacht skimmed rapidly between the shingle-banks piled on either side of the river-mouth at Shinglestreet, the ebb-tide was becoming parlously low, and her chances of negotiating the bar were ebbing with the tide. The whole system of the shingle-bank at the haven lay disclosed by the ebb, and she passed down the straggling range of it. One steep knoll (a great mound of shingle) ceased abruptly, and *there* was the open. At one moment there had been nothing but the wall-like shingle-bank, at next moment it was the open sea. Then another knoll piled up beside us, and we were again in a river. The pilot was on board. "Yes, you'll just about do it," he said, and the long low

REVENUE CUTTER, ORFORD, 1800

sea-line was over the bows. With both pairs of beacons aligned over her stern, the yacht was pointed seaward, and was chopping with a short pitch over the waves that broke on the bar. Round the yellow hills of shingle the sea-gulls scattered, hoarsely protesting, and again alighted. The pilot had gone. The movement of the yacht grew smoother and longer, and the haven began to dwindle astern. We were at sea.

. . . . . .

"But, Robinson," I said, "there's one thing you've missed. And I'm sorry."

It was this.

Seen as yet only in daylight, the old town had not received full justice. Somehow, a ramble over the grassy places in naked daylight could not quite discover the soul of it. The thing is better felt in a blur of twilight. That gaunt keep stands above it all, an impotent guardian over dead streets and depopulated water-ways. The old town was once there, and a mystery possesses the landscape still.

I was recalling a summer of a few years ago, telling my shipmate of it. But the sensation was one of "incommunicable dream," and I could not convince him. The wind, north-west, had been truculent during the day; in the twilight it was less rampant, and the yacht's anchor was brought on board. She was off Slaughden Quay. She filled away on her reefed mainsail, and streaked across the river with her swift grace of movement. The mainsheet was run out, the anchored vessels and the houses of Aldeburgh—blurred in the heavy blue twilight—had faded astern into distance; my shipmate and I were alone with the blown river-water and the stormy sunset.

So we sailed on until Orford loomed to westward of us. Nightfall followed on the heels of sunset, but full night was not upon us. That brownness of sundown lingered, and the Castle—a stern outline—stood squarely against it. The land lay in shadow. A blue haze, as of chimney smoke, hovered; but the houses were lost on the sombre land.

Sympathetically disposed, one can feel "the grandiose past affably real and near." Not withheld at moments like this, it becomes real and neighbourly. And each in our own fashion we dream our dreams.

Orford was ancient even before that Norman Castle stood squarely reared, and darkened against the sunsets of nearly eight hundred years ago. Centuries before that, the old sea-rovers haunted the river, the Danes sacked the town and defeated and killed Edmund at Haegelisdun (now perhaps Hollesley). Generations have trawled in the river and tilled the country-side. In endless procession they have passed and have slipped quietly into the shadows.

A bevy of fishermen, lusty and alive as the jerseyed fellows of to-day, would have been working on shipboard, hauling in their nets, when the famous wild man of Orford was captured. The story is told by Ralph of Coggeshall, and the date is said to have been 1204, in the reign of King John.

The fishermen saw the sea-monster writhing and sprawling in the meshes as the net came up. They kept him fast in the toils and sailed away for Orford. The creature resembled a man in size and figure, but the crown of his head was bald and his beard was long and ragged. He was given to the Governor of Orford Castle, whose servants "tied up the poor stranger by the heels and cruelly tormented him to make him speak." Another account says that he was tied up "to the smoke-jack" by his heels, and "as he could not be taught any Christian accomplishments" he was condemned to the turn-spit. He would sit by the settle by the fire-place, holding his head in his hands as if in pain. "He lay down on his couch at sunset and arose at sun-rise."

One day the fishermen

took him out in their boats, and, after spreading three rows of nets to prevent his escape, they allowed him to enter the water. He immediately dived under the nets and escaped to sea.

Bad as his treatment had been, however, his dread of the "smoke-jack" did not prevent his return. To the amazement of all Orford, he reappeared at the town. Of his own free will he again took his place by the settle; but at last he stole away to sea again, and finally disappeared.

That mediæval Orford from which he disappeared has itself now faded in the ages. Only, in the twilight, the Castle stands boldly against the sunset, and the town's shrunken vestige clusters below. The rest is memory and silence.

CHAPTER X

A CAPFUL OF WIND

"THE weather has been very patient with us so far," I was saying, "I thought she'd soon be giving us the rough side of her tongue."

Robinson screwed up his face as he listened to the *whoop* of a gust that whipped across, and we felt the yacht snub on her cable. We were at breakfast in the cabin.

"It would be the 'real thing' at sea to-day," he said wistfully. Then he tried to look ingratiating. "Couldn't we push out and have a look?" he pleaded.

But on that I was firm. No. No turn to windward against this for me, if *I* could anyway dodge it. I had blundered into this sort of thing unaware now and again, but I was not asking for gratuitous trouble.

He yielded graciously, as always. "This is useful experience," he was commenting, and I thought that he referred to the weather. But he was handling the tea-caddy. "I've never had housekeeping work before. But I thought that I couldn't really use a quarter of a pound of tea in one day, whatever my landlady said. I'll make the old bird toe the line when I get home."

We went ashore. *The Times* had an article on " June Gales ":

" The second day of the south-westerly type of weather," I read aloud, " has been marked by the occurrence of strong winds generally and of gales in places."

" That's us," Robinson interrupted.

" Gales in June," I continued reading, " are sufficiently rare to call for some comment when they occur, this month sharing with July the privilege of greatest immunity." I glanced lower down the column. " The forecasts issued by the Meteorological Office last evening point to a continuance of the same conditions."

My face lengthened, I dare say, for I had to get home in a day or two. " But it *must* blow itself out; it can't hold at this pace. Anyway, to-morrow we start, I want to get back to the Blackwater."

" Fine morning, I expect, after all this," he piously hoped, but I knew that his real desire was to see the weather keyed to this same pitch of riot and bluster.

. . . . .

Nor was he disappointed. Next morning the wind was almost as bad as ever—a moderate gale. But the sky looked healthier, and the wind would surely veer; there was time for improvement, seeing that the tide would not serve until three in the afternoon. The pilot would take us out at three.

So we made sail. Oilskinned and sou'-westered, we were away; we had dropped the pilot and were at sea.

" Not so bad," said Robinson, as the yacht lifted on the large green waves and slid into the trough. " She takes it first-rate."

" You lashed the fore-hatch, didn't you ? " was my only reply. I was conning over the rough-weather list in my mind—two painters on dinghy, fore-hatch and skylight fast, stoves and cabin furniture secured and all the other little items. We were still really under lee of the land, and I knew what was waiting for us. It was rough here, but we hadn't started yet.

Here it came, she was getting to it ; every wave was breaking, and the yacht trembled under the blow when the first big one fairly hit her. Green water rolled solid with its scurf of foam over the whole deck. The scuppers could not free her quickly enough, and the weight of water on the bulwark kept her down. She lifted gradually and was again flung down and pinned. The waves threw her, and the wind whistled and yelled. She would have her work cut out to make a haven to windward.

Robinson was jubilant. " I've never tasted this before," he said. And there certainly is a savage energy in wind and sea that gets into one's veins. One responds. On shore or on a large ship the thing is utterly different. But here, everything in one's little world is charged with it ; the waves rear beside and above one, the wind whips the foam from them and lays the boat almost on her beam-ends. The vigour is infectious. It is an orgy of noise and movement. The elements are loose.

A crash and jangle from the cabin showed that

Wette and colde can not make them

shrynke nor strayne
Whom ye North Sea hath dyed in grayne

AN OLD TAG OF THE SIXTEENTH-CENTURY SHIPMEN

my stowage—though conscientious—had not sufficed. Robinson poked his head inside and came out grinning. " It's bedlam let loose down there," he said, " and there's a river from the skylight."

He made a grab at the coaming as he spoke, his expression ludicrous. A sudden roll of the yacht, as some steep wave went under her, had almost knocked him headlong. He lurched and staggered, and again grabbed hold. " Drunk again," he spluttered as he blinked the water out of his eyes. " By Jove, it's a fact—' the pavement it come up an' 'it me in the eye! ' " He laughed. " I'd be groaning in a misery of sea-sickness on a steamer," he said, " but this is much too homely for that. I haven't given the thing a thought."

The green water *pounded* on board every time and washed to and fro on the deck. It swept the chain cable this way and that as if the iron links were no heavier than spun-yarn.

Then the tail of my eye caught a glimmer of unusual daylight in the cabin.

" Robin, quick," I shouted to him, " the fore-hatch." I shouted, though he was close beside me, for the wind tore one's words to tatters.

The fore-hatch had been lifted off bodily by the wash of the breaking seas. I could see the water surge round Robinson's sea-boots as he sprang for'ard along the deck, passing himself from runner to shrouds and clutching tight against the lurch and plunge of the little vessel. He had the cover down in an instant, and had gone below to secure it.

" Much water in ? " I asked, as he returned.

TURNING TO WINDWARD; TWO REEFS DOWN

" Not a great deal, I fancy. Good job you spotted it at the very instant." He breathed as if he had been running.

Again we settled ourselves, wedged tight in the well. And the noise of swirling water and breaking sea and shouting wind went on; it *drummed* upon our ears.

But it was almost over-strong; and no creature can endure exaltation beyond the ordinary for long together. If a rabbit is put into pure oxygen, the little animal pricks up its ears and frisks about delighted; its eyes sparkle with more than normal life. Then the phase passes, and it falls into gradual lassitude and so succumbs.

Exactly so it was with us. Robinson had been singing snatches of tune at first, but he too was feeling the wear and tear a little; merry of word still, he had ceased to sing.

" It's no use going on after the tide turns," I shouted to him, " we'll run into Harwich when we can get there, and anchor. We can get away again in the night."

He ducked his head to escape a deluge of foam, and then nodded. " I can't keep the water out," he grimaced, holding on hard again as the yacht lurched heavily to and fro, " it's down my neck every minute. But the thing is grand, it's monstrous, it's wonderful. I shall sleep to-night."

" You'll get four hours if you're lucky," I called back, as I put the helm down a little, luffing her into a high crest of greening white. It broke full on the bow, and then I bore away again.

We punched on. " Run into Harwich," I had said, but the harbour was still to windward, and night was not far off. I glanced up at the sails, and I looked down at the staunch little hull as she smashed through the seas. She was able and resolute enough now, but . . . Well, if anything vital carried away, I shouldn't attempt to bring her up this side of Orfordness, the first strip of weather-shore. There was no harbour available.

The very thought was a symptom, and nothing more; I recognised it.

" Reach out that hunk of bread and cheese that I left ready," I asked Robinson, and we were soon both munching great mouthfuls. " Keep the bread in shelter if you don't want it sopped," I said, and he laughed at my distended cheeks. Then a level cataract of spray made him shake his head like a dog does when it comes out of the water.

We were worlds better for the food, and real laughter returned. Felixstowe Pier was soon abeam, and we beat over the edge of the shoal-water. The seas were steep and vicious. The waves thudded. The spray swept and stung, but the end was in sight. I was rather glad of it, for a turn to windward on a day like this was something of a tax.

" Ease away the mainsheet," and we stood in past Landguard. Even inside, the sea was surprisingly rough, but we were off the wind now, and merely at our ease.

" We'll stand on up to Shotley in the Orwell; that's much the snuggest weather-shore." And there it was that we let go our anchor.

INTO THE NIGHT.

I pulled off my oilskins. " Now we'll have some grub," I said; " I'll get . . . Hul*lo* ! "

Robinson craned in over my shoulder into the cabin. He whistled, for the whole floor was awash.

" We didn't take that amount in through the hatch when it washed off," I told him; " I must have seen it long ago if we had." And I broke up the floor-boards of the well to look at the bilge. " She's sprung a leak."

We baled her out by the bucketful, which was much quicker than pumping. After considerable labour we got her empty, and I noted the time.

Robinson watched me narrowly; unable to assess

the degree of seriousness, he waited his cue, equally ready to laugh or to commiserate. I crawled through and set the stove going. " Cook the chops, like a good chap," I said, but he lingered for a fraction of a second.

" I can't tell yet," I explained; " the leak may take up of itself; turning to windward out there was a great strain on any boat, and she isn't young."

The water in the bilge was up to the floor-boards again. I took the time, and again baled it out; it was a long, long job—dozens of buckets.

" Thank goodness she didn't spring the leak earlier on," I thought, for she would have been water-logged and almost unmanageable in no time out there. I again emptied her, and the chops were now ready.

" Can we go on ? " Robinson asked, as we settled to the meal.

" I wonder," I replied; and we ate in silence.

When we looked at the bilge, however, the matter was hopeless. The water again was up to the floor-boards, and in shorter time than before. This was no manner of good, and I sighed heavily.

" Look at it," I protested, " the wind is steadying and the sky is better. We'll have a shift of wind that would give us a reach all the way to Mersea. And we can't go."

" No good ? " he questioned.

" We must get her up to Pin Mill and put her on the mud. We can't sit up all night pumping; and if we slept, she'd wake us up by going quietly to the bottom. But I shall sleep like a top when she's squatting on the dirt. Can't be helped," I added.

The tide was just turning against us, and it was slow work after Collimer Point was passed, although the reefs had been shaken out. Turning to windward in the dark over the ebb was an endless business, and we had to keep the lead going more than half the time. Then we had to empty the bilge. Again and again the tide set us back; but at last we were among the boats at Pin Mill, and we took the mud just to north of the causeway at midnight. The kedge was tossed overboard, and we were soon sound asleep. The tide would not reach her again until nearly seven in the morning. The mud till then was under her; securely aground, she could not sink if she tried.

CHAPTER XI

SEAWARD FROM ORWELL HAVEN

RETURNING to the yacht at Pin Mill one summer evening, we were again on board and the sails were on her. Repairs had been effected; all was ready, and the cable was being shortened to break out the anchor.

"It's a very dead pull; I don't like the feel of it," I commented uncomfortably.

Clearly we were foul of something. The tide was slipping seaward, and we were hung fast. One or two yachts, skimming lightly under sunlit sail, slid by and dwindled into distance; but we were held.

Then, peering over the bows, we spied the rusted flukes of a great anchor just below the surface. A further resolute pull brought a little more of our own chain up, but the rusty stranger—after lifting a little on the chain—slipped downward again along it.

"That's the fellow that's up to the mischief! Lucky we've brought the beggar up; now we've got to get a grip of him. No good shortening the cable, the big chap only slips down, and may slip once too often, right out of sight."

With a coil of rope, I was down in the dinghy,

THE BUTT AND OYSTER, PIN MILL

and, stretching under-water (sleeves, though rolled to the arm-pits, getting soused, as usual), had made two half-hitches firmly round the fluke.

"Together, haul." Back on board again, we hauled in unison; and with our last ounce of strength we hove the fluke over the rail and made it fast. Our own cable was unwound in a moment, and we were free of our captor.

A smack lay just below us, with one man on board. He had watched our doings with eyes that never blinked; his mates were fortunately ashore and had taken the boat, otherwise they would probably have been across to us, with all manner of advice.

We hailed him. "Are you anchored, or on a mooring?" I called.

He took his pipe out of his mouth. "Moorin',"

he said; "our anchor it lay out happen a bit shoreward o' you."

"Not a bit of it," I told him, with a grin. "The tiresome brute is on the rail here now. There it goes," I added (for by this time our own anchor was up and out of mischief), and with a huge splash the limpet-crusted stranger went plumb for the bottom.

The passage of by-play had consumed a thick slice of the early evening. We were now away, and the side-lights were being got ready; darkness would be on us before we reached the sea.

At the great mooring-buoys in mid-channel a barque was lying, and a flag at her masthead stood out, flat as a board, in the wind. Down here, the breeze was fluky and capricious, little gusts would gather and flutter out again in light airs. But it mattered nothing; we should slide away with the ebb. In a warmth of low sunlight we went.

Above Pin Mill is Chelmondiston, the square church tower of which is visible over the shoulder of the hill. The houses among the trees straggle down to the waterside.

Pin Mill has real charm. Its name and its position and its appearance suggest a long tale of old-world history; it seems a place where generations must have carried on their primitive business of the waterside since remote ages. So no doubt they have, but of the deeds and troubles which make history it has had little share. The old County Histories, lacking incident for record, will supply the names of former parsons and landowners of

PIN MILL · AND · CHELMONDISTON

Chelmondiston, but Pin Mill has not even that dignity. Its inhabitants have lived in the sunshine and watched the tides rise and fall; they have built their boats and sailed them, undisturbed, through the change of centuries. One reads, in a book published in 1830, of "a little inlet or creek, leading to a few straggling huts and cottages, called Pin Mill—where the weather-beaten fisherman and daring smuggler meet in friendly intercourse, to relate their hair-breadth escapes and wonderful adventures, over a pipe and a jug at the Butt and Oyster public-house." There is little more to be said. The coming of the yachts has made its inhabitants less unsophisticated, but otherwise Pin Mill remains as it was.

. . . .

We were leaving Pin Mill astern. The obelisk

·FRESTON·TOWER·

on the hillside is erected to the memory of William Berners, 1709–1783, "proprietor of Berners-Street, in London." But of less accountable origin is Freston Tower, higher up the river. Its object is not known; in 1655 it was presumed to be "part of a house lately built," and was possibly intended as a "view-point." It may also have been used for purposes of navigation, just as, upon Wherstead church tower, a mark was placed in some past century as a beacon for navigating the river.

Collimer Point was nearly abeam, and we were giving it a berth, remembering that long mud-spit which stretches, under water now, towards the big black buoy. Then the next reach opened. It was the straight fairway to Orwell Haven and the sea. Twilight was almost upon us.

BARGES · BOUND · SEAWARD · DOWN · THE · ORWELL

To north of us was a small creek, little known, which possesses its own shred of ancient history. At Levington Creek in 1801 a Roman urn was discovered, full of coins. There was possibly some Roman settlement there, the main traces of which have been long obliterated, and, in 1722, the creek assumed some importance in the eyes of Defoe for quite other reasons:

"In a creek, called Lavington Creek, we saw at low water such shoals, or hills rather, of mussels, that great boats might have loaded with them, and no miss have been made of them."

Seen from the river, it is just some deserted little corner, a backwater which through the centuries has looked out upon the changing traffic of the Orwell. Roman war-galley or Danish pirate, cog and carrack of the Middle Ages, or coal-brig of the later centuries, all have passed it and all have gone. Folk of the country-side and rough fishermen came and went; the boats, with creaking rowlocks, were pulled in, and mussels loaded in the days of Defoe, and there were songs and laughter when life was young.

> "Come, row the boat, row, to Levington Creek;
> The boat full of Roses as e'er it will stick.
> Row the boat, row,
> Yoho, yoho," etc. . . .

What it all relates to, one can hazard no notion. It sounds youthful and light-hearted, and the words still stand in some dusty book published a century ago. It was perhaps an old stave even then; a hundred years have passed over, and "all is at one now, roses and lovers."

"We'll get the side-lights up before we reach the traffic at Harwich." And my shipmate dropped down into the fo'c'stle.

On the eastern shore—a wooded pleasant land it looked in the twilight—lie the villages of Nacton and Trimley set back from the river. Nacton was the home of Admiral Vernon, and also of Sir Philip Broke, famous as captain of the frigate *Shannon*; Trimley was the home of Thomas Cavendish or Candish, an Elizabethan navigator, who sailed round the world shortly after Drake's famous voyage in the *Golden Hind*.

Vague, in the dusk to westward, was Shotley. Formerly known as Kirketon, this town had its market and fair since the days of Edward I, and Shotley-gate or Ferry (the ferry being over the

SHIPS OF KING ALFRED ENTERING
ORWELL HAVEN, A.D. 885

Stour) has been a main route between Harwich and Ipswich since the two towns have existed. Since they existed, also, the two towns were to some extent rivals. Ipswich was very jealous of Harwich, which, lying at the harbour-mouth, was able to levy port and harbour dues: in 1340, a commission was set up to inquire into the respective rights of the two towns, and the controversy lasted into the eighteenth century—a quarrel of four hundred years.

Into the seaward fairway of Harwich, with its glitter and snap of coloured lights, the yacht swam with her noiseless movement. It was southward into the night.

"Yes, we're back from the ruins and the desert. I see we are. There's nothing like this at Orford or Bawdsey." And my companion put the glasses on the dark form of a freighter of some tonnage which was at anchor. There was another cargo-steamer leaving, and sailing-barges were scattered about. "Yes, it's a contrast. This place is still alive."

Orwell Haven has been consistently important. Every generation has come to it. The Danes, needless to say, made full use of the haven in their day. Easily entered and wholly secure, it was an anchorage after their own heart. A terror to the country-side, the pirates came as they pleased; they sacked and burnt, and—based always upon the sea—they had swift retreat available from superior force.

Military measures were powerless against sudden descents and discreet withdrawals. Clumsily floundering on a marshy coast-line, a whole burnished and bannered army could only shake its fists at the marauders, who, sitting undisturbed in their ships, could overhaul their plunder within sight and hail of the shore. Only by sea-power could our shores be rightly screened, and Alfred the Great was our first admiral of defence. About the year 885 his war-galleys descended upon the confident Danes in Orwell Haven; sixteen of their ships were taken and destroyed, and—with grim promptitude—every prisoner was put to the sword.

The yacht was entering the haven.

Merit as an anchorage has given Orwell Haven an important place in history.

"This is a very safe Harbour; and if a Ship should chance to blow ashoar, she cannot take any harm, the shoars being soft Owse."

If her cables parted outside, she would drive helplessly upon some wave-beaten lee-shore or shoal, and become a total wreck; in the haven she would merely drive upon the soft mud, and refloat unscathed after the trouble. The anchorage had, moreover, ample space and depth. It is recorded that upwards of 100 sail of war with frigates, and between 300 and 400 colliers, were riding here at the one time without endangering one another. For these reasons the haven became the foremost port of Suffolk. The Deben and Ore were prejudiced by their shallow bars, the Blyth was of little account, and Lowestoft and Yarmouth were unable to accommodate the largest ships. Hence Orwell Haven was pre-eminent.

"I'm afraid I'm disenchanted," said Robinson. "The place is brimmed with wonders, it's full of history; full as you please of 'whispers and of shadows.' But I've lost the magic somehow. It's all usual and expected, in spite of the twilight and afterglow and everything else."

Landguard Fort lay on the port bow, and he eyed it with some disfavour. It looked prosaic. "Landguard was once a regular island for a time," I told him. And I recounted how, in 1569, there was a breach to the north of it, through which the sea was washing freely. The new inlet set up a deflection of the tides in the estuary, and the silt thrown up began to threaten the very existence of Ipswich as a seaport.

In 1587, the year before the Armada, the authorities were frankly disturbed, for the shores were so steep as to offer every facility for landing; and the enemy, once established, would be difficult to dislodge.

My shipmate warmed to it a little. "I can fancy that, and Seymour's ships here, after the Armada, and so on. Yes, it's the same harbour."

"Shift your fancy a bit later and I've got a yarn for you," I said. It is small, but here it is.

The Commandant at Landguard was able to dominate the haven with his guns, and was monarch of all he surveyed. When a King's ship in 1629 put into Harwich Harbour, he sent word to the captain to strike his flag. The captain, a King's officer, declined with some heat; whereupon the soldier sent word that he would sink the offender,

LORD HENRY SEYMOUR'S SHIPS IN THE ROLLING GROUND, AFTER DEFEAT OF THE ARMADA, 1588

as he "had warrant from my Lord of Warwick to do so." Holding the King's commission, the captain was contemptuous: "I slighted that authority," he said, "and replied that I thought myself as able to beat their paper fort to pieces with my ordnance as they to sink me, and bade them take heed how they made the first shot."

A KING'S SHIP OF THE DUTCH WARS

Unfortunately there the story ends; the final issue is wanting. Shots were evidently exchanged and some damage done, but, whether the flag or fort came down, history has no word.

Then, in 1666, the Dutch attacked Landguard. A favourite anchorage of the Dutchmen in those evil days was inside the Gunfleet Sand, and "ye buoy of ye Gunfleete," at N.E. end of the shoal, was more than once removed by the port authorities for that reason. The coast towns lived in a state of trepidation when the Dutchmen furled their sails and let go their hempen cables in the Wallet. Where would they attack?

The question was not long in doubt on this occasion, for the guns began to play upon Landguard Fort. About three thousand men were landed, but they were

LANDGUARD POINT·

AT ORWELL HAVEN

ye Katharine of ye Tower ankerd in ye Orwel haven mcxxxv

powerless against the massive walls, and — if there had been real initiative on our side—they might have been cut off to a man. As it was, they re-embarked at Felixstowe, and the great ships, masterfully moving through our own shoal-waters, set sail. In splendid array they laid their course north-eastward, but three of them went aground—one after another—on the Whiting Shoal, off Orford Haven. They were refloated without loss.

From 1702–4 Captain Richard Steele, friend of Addison, was in command at Landguard. It is a small link, but not without interest.

The steam ferry crossed our track, with her crowded complement of passengers, and a tug-boat from Harwich was butting through the dark water with a heavy bow-wave.

Here then was Orwell Haven.

> "For *Orwell* comming in from *Ipswitch* thinks that shee
> Should stand for it with *Stour*, and lastly they agree,
> That since the Britons hence their first discoveries made,
> And that into the East they first were taught to trade,
> Besides of all the Roads and Havens of the East,
> This Harbour where they meet is reckoned for the best."

This was what Drayton said in 1613.

The last rhyme would perhaps be assessed by Walker's Rhyming Dictionary as an "allowable rhyme." It is far from perfect, and it suggested to Robinson, moreover, an unfortunate gloss, which must not be indulged. He jeered at Drayton's overgrown lines, preferring the simple words of the *Breviary of Suffolk*, published five years later:

"Orwel never ceaseth vntill it drowneth it selfe in the bottomlesse well in the mouth of the Haven named of old from the said ryver Vrewell haven, butt in these dayes Orewell haven.

"Stour sheddeth it selfe into the Flemmish Ocean between Harwich and Orwell haven."

The name given to the North Sea is interesting. It was with the Flemings that our east coast traded in the Middle Ages, and their ships plied to our ports from across the "Flemmish Ocean." Broad-beamed and cumbersome, the old carracks rolled back the foam from bluff bows as they entered Orwell Haven; the great mainsail was clewed up, and, with shouts and bustle, the brawny shipmen made ready to anchor. Gladly enough they made their haven with a rich cargo unrifled. The high seas were full of pirates, and peaceful commerce by sea a speculative venture.

Even in port, however, ships were not entirely safe. Pirates would swoop in from the open sea outside, and would be away again before authority could catch them. But the limit was reached when the very policeman turned burglar, and the shepherd took the habit of the wolf. In 1315 a Cinque Ports ship, which had been specially commissioned to protect commerce against piracy, entered Orwell Haven and barbarously plundered two peaceful Flemish ships lying at anchor in the port. Similarly, in the reign of Queen Elizabeth, the Vice-Admiral of Essex, despatched to cruise after pirates, turned pirate himself and came to a bad end.

Not always operating singly, the pirates were even more formidable when combined in a small fleet. In 1335 four ships, all manned by Englishmen, entered the Orwell. Literally for three months they remained in undisputed possession; they terrorised the place, they plundered and sank all the trading vessels, and held the crews to ransom. They even detained ten ships which had been prepared for the Royal Service. It was an effort which seems to have vindicated its own impudence by its complete success.

In 1405 we find a King's ship *Katharine of the Tower* detailed to lie in Orwell Haven; she was there to protect shipping against the French who were raiding the coast, not against pirates.

Then, more than a century later, Henry VIII came down to Harwich, determined to stop this piracy which was sapping the vitals of our commerce. Any ship, ostensibly a peaceful trader, was

A SHIP OF ANSON'S

apt to turn buccaneer if opportunity offered, and then to resume her rôle of peace and virtue when convenient; the risks were becoming so high that even the most daring merchants would soon cease to speculate. Henry VIII introduced the regulation and registration of ships, their inspection and certification. Slowly, from these beginnings, our ordered and regulated mercantile marine emerged, protected by the Royal Navy, whether in peace or war.

In 1596 half a dozen Dunkirkers were blockading Harwich, and nearly thirty traders were taken. Privateering was especially rampant after the defeat of the main fleets of any antagonist; no longer able to oppose successful force of arms, the worsted enemy preyed upon our commerce. In war after war the same thing has occurred.

It was a perfect night to be afloat. The cool breeze was steady and the sea smooth. Clear of Landguard Point we had opened the Cork Light and were away for Essex once more.

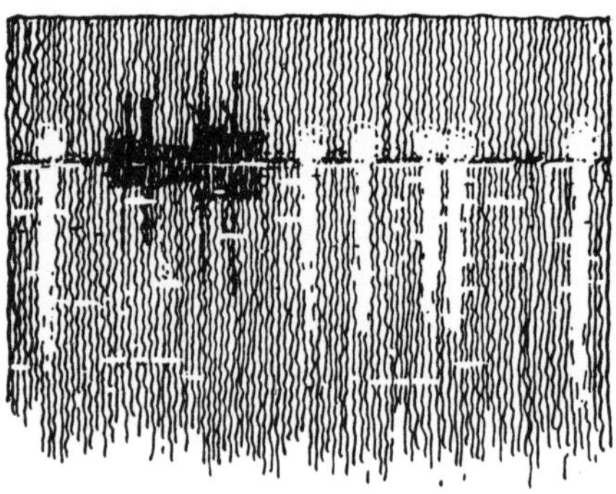

CHAPTER XII

TO IPSWICH IN GREY WEATHER

GREY light had perhaps begun to temper the cloud-banks outside, but it had not penetrated into the cabin. Night was unbroken here; the alarm-clock alone was responsible for the idea that it was morning.

The yacht was back in Essex, anchored in the Colne, off East Mersea, and opposite the mouth of Brightlingsea Creek.

"Rouse out," I called, but my shipmate had no such intention.

"Wh-y?" he queried at immense length, for a yawn had caught the word in the middle. He paused, for he was again yaw-haw-haw-hawning. "Why? 'Tisn't morning yet," he asserted with a sense of grievance. "*Is* it?" he pleaded with a sudden change of tone.

He sat up. "What's the glass doing?"

"Fallen two-tenths. Blowing stiff, and raining a little."

"Anything else in the little catalogue of virtues?" and he threw aside the blankets.

I had already put the kettle on for a cup of coffee. We would eat an atom of cold breakfast underway. The tide had been emptying seaward for more than an hour already, and we wanted the ebb along the coast.

Down seaward the light of Colne Point was still flashing in the grey; and rain—with a renewed scatter—whipped across one's face. Our oilskins were shining with it.

Clouds were sullen enough in the half-light as they swept unceasingly northward, and the seascape was grey and unhappy. I glanced at the cabin clock before I went for'ard to get up the anchor; the time was just four.

The anchor was soon clanking against the bob-stay. Up went the reefed mainsail, and we were away. It was a beat, with long leg and short, down to the Point; after that her wind would be free. She was bound for the Orwell and Ipswich.

The waves ridged up, foam-crested, as they bore landward against the tide; it was a dirty morning. Rain again swept over awhile and then slackened. "Lee-ho," and she was about.

Opening the deeper water, clear of Mersea shore, she threw the spray in clouds. She lurched and she staggered. As she crested the wave and flopped awkwardly over, the next wave—breaking beyond it—caught her and buried her. The deck swam with green water. She rose again, and it streamed off her, away through the lee scuppers. *Swash!* And another green cargo was sluicing over the battened fore-hatch.

Faces and oilskins alike were streaming; but this baptism would soon be over. Level with the Point, we should ease away her mainsheet for her, and

—off the wind—she would run coastwise, dry as a bone.

Cloud-colour was unrelieved; and this rebellious seaway, as it frothed and bubbled, was wearing its dirtiest tinge of sullen green. The mainsheet was running out through the blocks. She was free; the wind was on her quarter.

"Wet enough for a beginning. Put her on a wind, and old Noah's deluge isn't in it." Robinson laughed as he loosened his oilskin collar; and we watched the flat coast-line slipping away astern of us.

"Shan't be long getting to Clacton Pier. There's not much of the colour of the railway-posters about. Look at it."

There was not. Cold-grey, blurred with driven rain, the town and pier looked a picture of desolation. The pier-head was soon abeam, and was left—with the restless tumult of waves that threshed themselves white about it—to leeward. We were moving at speed.

Sound of a sharp snap jerked us out of our mood of contentment. The dinghy was adrift. Lurching and toppling off in the rough seaway, it had gone.

"I thought as much. It's our own fault: in the dark we forgot that second painter."

We luffed the yacht round, and put her on the wind. The seaway was one long range of foam-caps as we looked to windward, every wave of them trying to ruffle and bluster. A puny little atom the lost dinghy looked, strayed away in all that tumult.

It is an easy task enough to come up beside a lost dinghy; the difficulty is to get her in tow. The relative positions of yacht and dinghy register the depth of the lift and plunge, and one finds it considerable. The chance of getting thrown into the ditch one's self while trying to secure the truant is no remote contingency. Three times over we had to hunt her before we got her on a painter again. Then we pinioned her and twin-paintered her and brought her properly to heel.

Away we went for Harwich. The orthodox course for larger vessels leads in from the other side of the Gunfleet Sand. The mariner was warned, in *Great Britain's Coasting Pilot* of 1692, that, on account of the tide, "especially in little wind or calms, you may be hauld on the Sand," and the correct course was thus interpreted:

"Being in the Rowling-grounds, and that you would sail into *Harwich* Harbour, keep close by the *Andrews*, which is a Sand that lyeth off *Landguard-Fort*, and is steep too on the west side; the Tyde of Ebb runneth strong over the *Andrews* the first half Ebb, of which you must have a care; this sand is dry at low-water."

The directions are still sound, but the sand has ceased to uncover. Other sands dry out, conscientiously enough, at every ebb; but not the Andrews. Never, for a century or so, has it had less than four feet of water, even at Springs.

"Constant change going on?" my shipmate said. "The tide hollows fresh ways through the sand. Just as the little pools and channels on the beach used to change, every tide almost, when one was a kid."

It is a controversial point, but the changes have not

NELSON'S "MEDUSA"

been drastic during the few centuries of which we have certain knowledge. One channel may gradually shoal and another gradually open, but the process is slow.

Long before the northward tidal current along the coast had exhausted itself we were entering Harwich Haven against the ebb. The Bell-buoy, clanging in the turbulent channel, was astern, and we were making good our passage to the River Orwell.

" Orwell " it is now, but in Saxon annals it figured as " Arwan " or " Arwell." The river gave its name

DUTCH FLY-BOATS TAKEN IN THE WAR . . . WHICH COST NOTHING BUT THE CAPTION.
DEFOE. 1722

to the towns of Arwerton and Arwich. In the case of the latter town, hard-breathing generations have blown stoutly upon the "A," so that the pronunciation is now "Harwich."

Defoe, when he reached Harwich during his tour of 1722, sent his horses round by Manningtree, "where there is a timber bridge over the Stour, called Cataway Bridge," and himself took boat up to Ipswich. "Orwell" he called the river, but he did so with apologies to local usage. "A traveller will hardly understand me" (he said), "especially a seaman, when I speak of the River Stour and the River Orwell, for they know them by no other names than those of Manningtree Water and Ipswich Water."

Of Ipswich, formerly eminent in shipbuilding, Defoe spoke regretfully. In his view the Dutch wars had been the cause of its undoing.

Dutch fly-boats taken in the wars, " which cost nothing but the caption, were bought cheap, carried great burthens, and the Ipswich building fell off for want of price, and so the trade decayed, and the town with it."

It was a pity, for Ipswich had been accustomed to build the colliers for the Newcastle–London trade, and " they built there so prodigious strong " that the ships were long-lived beyond the ordinary.

That coal trade, carried in brigs mostly, was a picturesque feature of the coast. There were brigs by the hundred, and the skill and address with which they were handled among a press of shipping were proverbial. The skippers, moreover, were paid by the voyage, and were therefore jealous of time. It was no case of " more days, more dollars " with them; and they drilled their crews into the smartest crews afloat.

Londoners evidently then bought their coals at " lowest summer prices," for the collier's trade was a summer trade only, and the ships were laid up in winter. Here is Defoe's account:

" In the winter-time . . . the coal trade abates at London, the citizens are generally furnished, their stores taken in, and their demand is over; so that the great ships, the northern seas and coast being also dangerous, the nights long and the voyage hazardous, go to sea no more, but lie by " (*i.e.* here in the Orwell), " the ships are unrigged, the sails, etc. carried ashore, the topmasts struck, and they ride moored in the river, under the advantages and security of sound ground, and a high woody shore, where they lie as safe as in a wet dock; and it was a very agreeable sight to see perhaps two hundred sail of ships, of all sizes, lie in that posture every winter. All this while, which was usually from Michaelmas to Lady Day, the masters lived calm and secure with their families in Ipswich."

That description related to the year 1687; in 1722 the part borne by Ipswich in the coal trade had so far declined that "there were now scarce forty sail of good colliers that belonged to the whole town."

The beauty of the river, with its wooded banks, has always been matter for comment. There is a gracious quality in the landscape of all its reaches. Thomas Gainsborough knew every haunt of it. Forced by contemporary taste to concentrate upon the painting of portraits, his earlier love was for landscape. He painted repeatedly beside the Orwell.

But his generation had no love for landscape work. As Sir William Beechey recorded, these canvases of Gainsborough's "stood ranged in long lines from his hall to his painting-room, and they who came to sit to him for their portraits rarely deigned to honour them with a look as they passed by."

But Robinson was not thinking of Gainsborough.

"What's the little packet moored on the starboard side?"

The yacht had passed Shotley Spit buoy, and the little vessel to which my shipmate referred was the pilot-boat.

"With buoys at every twist of the whole waterway?" he protested. "Pilot? Surely that's rather a refinement? Useful sort of skipper he'd be who

IPSWICH COLLIER-BRIGS, OR "GEORDIES"
(EIGHTEENTH AND NINETEENTH CENTURIES)

couldn't put his little bag-of-tricks up this little trickle himself."

He had not given sufficient credit to the port of Ipswich, with its trade and its spacious wet docks. These pilots know the configuration of the river-bottom, and—with a ship of some tonnage—the very inches count. In less skilled hands she might stick immovably in one of the reaches; and would perhaps be surrounded, next high tide, by hopeful activities, with a tug or two in attendance—endeavouring to haul her off her mud berth into the channel.

Great efforts have been made by the town of Ipswich to maintain and enhance its natural advantages as a port. In the year 1805 an Act was passed for "improving and rendering more commodious the port of Ipswich." The deep-water channel was widened and many thousand tons of soil were taken from the bed of the river. Then, in 1825, a company of enterprising business men in Ipswich thought of trying steam; and the Ipswich Steam Navigation Company was launched, for conveyance of goods and passengers to London. Though deserving of a better fate, the company failed, and its steamboats were sold at a heavy loss.

"Here comes the River Packet."

As the yacht reached up towards Collimer Point, the double-ended, yellow-funnelled packet hove into view, her paddle-wheels slap-slap-slapping the water into a white wake of foam. Close beside our track she steered, shaping course for Harwich. We lifted over the first wave of her wash, and plunged—almost

TRAMP STEAMERS AT IPSWICH

bowsprit-under—into the next. The wash is one of the impressive features of the packet-service. The waves ridged away shoreward, and ran breaking along the low spits of tidal bank.

" That wash can be quite a nuisance further up," I was saying, for at low water there isn't too much room, and I have heard of yachts (sailing close inshore to give the steamer room in the narrows) being lifted momentarily shoreward by the wash—only to find themselves, as it receded, fast aground.

With a falling tide the yacht must sit there till the flood-tide comes up to the rescue.

The regular service between Ipswich and Harwich has existed for years, even centuries. A century ago the packets were under sail, and started from Ipswich—not by the clock, but according to the state of the tide. Thus in 1830, for instance, it was stated that " the wherry or passage-boat leaves the Quay daily, so as to take advantage of the tide." Sometimes, however (as the contemporary writer admitted), " from lack of wind, the passage may be tedious."

The yacht was now past Pin Mill, and was herself reaching those narrower waters. She had romped past the few sailing vessels with which she could match herself and a couple of spritsail barges were now ahead. Confidently she foamed along their wake and drew even. It was a reaching wind. The old barge-master, casting an eye aloft at his bellied top-sail, ran the spokes of his wheel round, luffing her a little more towards the weather-shore. He was hugging it as tight as ever we could have dared; there was to be no passing of him to windward.

" Bear away, and have a shot. But his sails will blanket us; I doubt whether we'll carry through so close under his lee."

Heeling gracefully from the wind, the yacht cut swiftly through the water; overhauling her, hand over fist, the yacht was close beside the barge, level with her helmsman. But our sails were a-quiver, and we were spilling all our speed. She had taken our wind.

" Dirty morning outside." We were both just in from the sea and were now sailing side by side. And we exchanged one or two more friendly commonplaces before we luffed right into the wind, and let the barge draw ahead. Then we charged down upon her again; one little fluky breath of wind at the right moment would have brought us through as we hung on the very verge of success; but no. At the third time of asking we slipped right through, and also took her consort in our stride. We had left the two of them astern.

Comely objects they had looked as we went by them. The shape of the brown sails, those dark brown sails hollowed and curved by the wind, was really good; and each square-cut barge-master, a short-coated figure, stood at his wheel, getting the very last ounce out of his ship. Thin smoke, blowing from a short chimney, told of a fire in the cabin below. And behind the brown sails rose the wooded landscape.

In Downham Reach, " ships of almost any burden " could " ride secure." It was in the old days when those lines of Crabbe's would have been applicable here:

> " Far other craft our prouder river shows,
> Hoys, pinks and sloops, brigs, brigantines and snows."

But even now, at the mooring-buoys below Pin Mill, tall barques and barquentines may be seen lying with barges about them, transferring cargo. Brigs and brigantines—so far as these waters are concerned—must be well-nigh extinct; and the iron

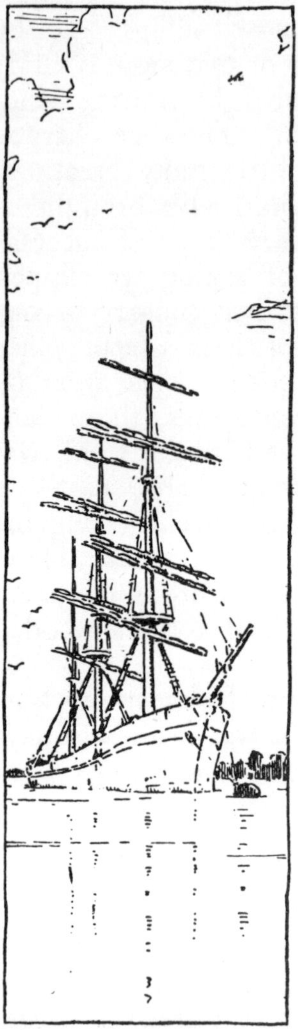

BARQUE MOORED IN THE ORWELL.

steamboats with their painted funnels are the boats that thresh purposefully up to Ipswich Docks. They have almost ousted sail. But they in turn will perhaps be chased from the sea-ways; even less dignified and attractive, the flush-decked, featureless hull of the motor ship may follow.

With a romping wind today the yacht was paying little heed to the fact that the tide was still contrary. The wide flats were uncovered.

"Looks forsaken enough," Robinson said. "Think of it under a blue sky, at high tide, and then—this." His comprehensive glance at dull sky and dreary distance condemned everything. "*What* a day!"

Another scurry of rain had evoked the protest. Ordinarily, even at low water, the tidal river does not forgo its charm, but this cloud and driven rain would vitiate any landscape under heaven. We turned up the collars of our oilskin coats.

"Yes," he continued ruminatively, "I rather think the cabin has its points to-day. A pipe, a book, a pair of carpet slippers—and I'm not sure that a glass of grog doesn't come into the picture. We were up before four, after all."

Ipswich was over the bows. The long tidal flat that stretched away to Bourn Bridge and the old "Ostrich" Inn was on our port hand; running the mainsheet right out, we headed her for the anchored shipping and the stone walls of Ipswich Docks. The channel was clear. We swept up it at a fury of speed, right up to the dock-gates, then sent the yacht into the wind, and brought up beside a mooring-buoy, dead-still. We moored in the tier, and got the canvas off her at our leisure. We felt as if it were afternoon; in reality, the time was half-past ten.

The carpet-slippers were not in service for long. We idled perhaps an hour or two, looking out from time to time to see the barges which, lower down the river, we had outstripped. One by one they brought up near the dock-gate, and were warped alongside somewhere or other—out of the way—until it was time for the gates to open. Then we pulled on our boots again. Leaving the dinghy at the steps by the dock-gate, we climbed a ladder and went ashore.

Opposite was the old quay, the "Common Quay" as it was called. That, no doubt, was where the "ducking-stole" (which still exists) was used in the old days, to the joy of some motley crowd, assembled at the waterside. In the year 1597, for instance, three women, condemned as "scolds," were ducked—"a salutary warning to those who may be apt to indulge too freely in licentious volubility of speech."

The Common Quay itself—at least once in its history—has been under water as well. In March of the year 1828 "an extraordinary high tide overflowed the Common Quay." The wind had been blowing a gale from the north-west, and—two hours before the regular time of high tide—the water was "near five feet higher than a regular spring tide."

Ipswich is a place of which one finds it difficult to form a single impression. The town appears less of a considered entity than many of its fellows—possibly because there is no outstanding building that dominates it, a Cathedral or some great and ancient castle. It impresses one as diffuse, uncertain, impersonal.

Yet it has its greatness and its history. After the Romans, the Saxons had their settlements here; and then, in 991, the Viking long-boats came up on the flood-tide of the Orwell, and the place was sacked and burnt. But it renewed its life. Its natural advantages as a port were obvious. Named "Gyppeswic," after Gipping River on which it stood, it appears in the Domesday Book. It held its royal charters from the Plantagenets. It was a port of note, with its own ships. King Edward III demanded twelve ships from it for his siege of Calais

SHIP OF IPSWICH, 1450

and so—through reign after reign—its history continued, a proud town of the Middle Ages.

In 1471 its greatest townsman was born—Cardinal Wolsey. The controversy is still maintained as to whether the Cardinal's father was really a butcher or not. The average opinion seems to be that the elder " Wulsy " (for so he wrote his name) was a burgess of Ipswich whose interests touched the butchery trade among other things, and that he was not merely the fifteenth-century counterpart of our own tradesman with a

IPSWICH

striped apron. The question, after all, is hardly important.

A man of Wolsey's genius, born as he was in a seaport town, might be expected to have had some real vision in the matter of sea-power. But the reverse was the case. Henry VIII ("Rex meus") was alive to it, but Wolsey's bias was always towards the land.

Ipswich ships played their part in the defeat of the Armada; then, after the Spaniards, the Dutch became the national enemy, and Oliver Cromwell organised the nation's resources to real purpose. The Protector's iron hand was felt everywhere. His orders to Ipswich, for an embargo on shipping or for impressment of seamen, brooked no delay. They would be endorsed:

Hast.
Hast.
Post Hast.

Or more urgently still:

Hast.
Post Hast.
Hast on your Life.

The Commonwealth ships not only attacked the Barbary pirates of the Mediterranean and released the Christian galley-slaves, but—of more importance to the east coast of England—they drove off the foreign pirates who used to prey upon our harbours, sometimes carrying off fishing-boats from the very rivers.

One must not linger unduly, but the hogs of mediæval Ipswich are certainly worth mention. In the reign of King Edward IV, the habit of keeping hogs was so popular in Ipswich that special orders were needed to regulate the "swinish multitude," as they were called in the preamble. Indignant townsmen who found a neighbour's hog rooting up the garden need no longer be content with driving it off; the hog trespassing and discovered in the fact might be seized and sold; the aggrieved citizen would then halve the proceeds, half for his own pocket and half for the coffers of the town.

Then, in the evolution of a century or two, the town was no longer a general pig-sty, but so cleanly as to call for John Evelyn's special comment. In 1677 he wrote that "it is for building, cleanness and good order one of the best towns in England." In 1722 Defoe wrote to the same purpose, tabulating its virtues, and recommending it as a place of retreat "for families who have lived well, but may have suffered in our late calamities of stocks and bubbles."

We, on this grey day, were now prowling about Ipswich Docks. The modern town has important industries, including the manufacture of agricultural machinery, railway plant, manures, oil-cake, and so on.

We had talked airily of the cabin and carpet-slippers; but, as usual, we had spent the daylight hours in the open. Rain or no rain, we had wandered round Ipswich; and now, at four in the afternoon, it was high water. We went back on board. At five we were making ready to set sail.

"Droppin' down to Pin Mill?"

I looked up from the traveller-outhaul; a burly fellow was in a row-boat, resting on his oars.

"Yes," I said. "Want a tow?"

"No, no, I ain't a-goin' down, not to-night." He had only paused to gossip, and I accommodated him.

"Ain't much room to turn to wind'ard out o' that little berth," he commented, voicing my own thoughts, for the wall of the Quay was close opposite, and the wind dead foul. "Now two gen'lemen," he continued with relish, "they started off two-three nights ago, same's you. Ebb tide; they said they was goin' to Pin Mill. *Said* they was goin', but they didn't git there; tell you for why. Took the mud and dried out."

Then he pulled away a little distance, and again rested on his oars. He wanted to see us go. If the bowsprit snapped against the wall, for instance,

(ARMS OF IPSWICH)

or wedged itself in the rigging of some moored vessel, he would feel repaid for sitting in the rain to watch. But he remained unsatisfied. Each time that the helm was put down, Ipswich had fallen further astern.

There was a hard breeze, and rain. We beat out in a tumult of water.

" Look at the squall," I shouted, " there's a black 'un."

With eye to windward I had seen it coming; the edge of the heavier rain was lashing the water into smoke and a tearing wind had thrown it upon us in an instant. Luffed for a moment to judge the weight of the squall, the yacht bore away again confidently, and carried on. The rain was in torrents, and the wind put the lee-rail under.

" It's gone."

The wind, which had blown full-bodied all day, had gone in an instant. There was a flat calm. Not a breath was stirring, and we could hear the drip, drip, drip of the rain from our oilskins. The water, foam-crested a moment ago, was swiftly settling to a level lake, pitted only by the still falling raindrops.

Then a faint breath quickened again. It had veered to north-west, a fair wind for us; and, as it did so, the sunshine leaped out with a living glitter. Full in our eyes it shone, and the tree-clad slopes to eastward had suddenly contrived, with the dark cloud above them, a living harmony of transparent green and grey. It was a magical moment.

With the fair wind we carried on past Pin Mill,

AT NIGHTFALL

and brought up off Shotley. Bound seaward to-morrow, we were well on our way. The breeze again flattened out; and—in the cool twilight which followed—the surface of the water became a perfect mirror. A thin mist, rising from its surface, enhanced the sense of quietude and isolation.

"Well, well," said Robinson, with something like a sigh, "I'm sorry we've finished."

CHAPTER XIII

LANDLOCKED WATERS

BUT we had not quite finished. A week later we had taken the train to Lowestoft.

" Fresh water here," Robinson said. He dipped his finger overside and put it to his lips. " Hardly brackish at all, anyway."

Here was a change of scene: we were on Oulton Broad. We had debated when at sea off Gorleston a week or two back whether to bring the yacht in; but I had decided to hire. *Irene* would be too slow in stays for the Broads; one requires a boat which will go about in her own length. So here we were.

" It's a pond," said Robinson, " and toy-boats on it." The idea did not last, but it was a first impression, as he looked round at the level water between grassy shores, and the crowd of white boats.

" Let's get on with the job," I said (it was seldom that *he* need be stimulated to energy), " the wind is fair; let's get out of this."

" Hear, hear," he applauded, and we made sail.

This latest expedition of ours was needed to complete the exploration of Suffolk sea-borders. Thrust up into Norfolk, there is a queer tongue of land which—in owning allegiance to Suffolk—declares itself a relic of time gone by. Here at Oulton

Broad, by Lowestoft, we were entering the River Waveney, and that river, narrow enough now, was once a broad tidal estuary. This tongue of land was practically islanded by the sea; it was—in the days of Queen Elizabeth—known as the Isle of Lovinge Land: "The main sea environeth the said island." Camden spoke of it, in the same reign, as "a pretty large peninsula, called by some Lovingland," and his description was probably the more literal of the two, as it is unlikely that a real outlet existed here. The name Lovingland has since, by a curious transition, reached its own antithesis, "Lothingland."

Before coming on board to-day we had ranged about the busy Lowestoft streets and the harbour-side. I had quoted with relish another passage from Camden's *Britannia:* "At the entrance, Leostoff, a little town, hangs (as it were) over the sea." "A little town," by the standards of Queen Elizabeth's reign, must have been really little; and now—"Well, look at it," as Robinson said. "Old Camden would rub his eyes, and wonder what the bigger places like Orford and Aldeburgh had grown to by this time."

This was a fair wind; with a slight sense of relief we had left Oulton Broad, entering the narrow dyke that connects it with the Waveney. We were out in the country, clear of everything. "Really," Robinson was saying, "it's a sort of pastoral afloat"; and he looked with appreciation at the rushes that nodded all along the border of the stream. "It's a wonderful change," he said.

LOWESTOFT TRAWLERS (AT FOOT: ARMS OF LOWESTOFT)

The little yacht was of the usual " Broads " type — of shallow draught, with a lifting cabin-top, and quick in stays. At present we had no occasion to try her powers, for her wind was free; when she opened the Waveney, she made slow work of it, for the flood-tide was streaming in and the wind was light. " Same factors still, tidal water and wind," Robinson said, a little ponderously for him, and then, with a touch of his own self: " But everything in a glass case," he added. " This is what I call the quiet life."

Clearly we should not get far this evening, for the sun was already low in the sky. " Still, it doesn't matter," as Robinson was prompt to observe, " when you've had enough, *you just stop*. Never mind where you are. No haven to find, no barometer to bother about; well, there's comfort about it, anyway. Never a spice of worry, I should fancy, here."

As he spoke, a yacht

SUNSET ON THE WAVENEY

LANDLOCKED WATERS

approached us which was oddly spasmodic in her movements, for she fouled one bank, and then found herself taken aback — so that there were mutual shoutings on board her, and furious shoving with a quant-pole. "*That's* the spice of worry here," I confided in a whisper, "the duds. They'll blunder into us next." And we watched with anxiety until — with their own eccentric progress—they had contrived a passage across, and we could slip past their stern. One of the two lads looked hot and harassed, the other was grinning from ear to ear; it just was a matter of temperament. Both were incompetent, but one took it to heart and meant to do better; the other was perfectly happy to make a fool of himself, here or elsewhere.

"Did I make the ship look as drunk as that when I started?" asked Robinson, out of countenance for the moment at the thought of it. "Perhaps, even now, I wouldn't be any better in these ditches," he added, with sudden misgiving.

I hastened to reassure him. True, he had the advantage of sea-room when a beginner, but he had instinct, which counts for so much more. Some men smell trouble from a mile off, and blunder helplessly into every scrape possible; but some, like Robinson, have the instinct for doing the right thing rightly. If he were a coal-heaver, he would heave his coals with accuracy; if he were a ploughman, his furrow would be the straightest on earth, and all the clods of all the country would not rob his figure of its native poise.

None of which, needless to mention, was said aloud. I merely played the heavy father, with a spice of banter which was good for his soul.

"What's the red flag?" he asked in a moment. "Rifle range?"

I had not noticed it until he spoke, but there it was, over the land. Allowing for the bends of the river, it must be the flag at the railway bridge at Somerleyton. The bridges here are swing-bridges, and a red flag is shown when they are closed to the river; when the bridge swings open, down comes the flag.

The tide seemed to run more strongly, and the wind was weakening with sundown. It was just sunset-time when we were approaching the bridge, and we saw the flag go down. A yacht was beating up-river, helped by the swift tide; a contrast to her precursor, she was handled with certainty and address. She lost her wind, perhaps, at the bridge, but the tide swept her through, and she passed us as we slowly made the entrance.

The tide was bubbling past the piers; and our little yacht, after carrying gamely in, lost her wind too, and stopped in mid-stream, barely holding her position against the running flood. The signalman —who had been perturbed at our entry—was now in a panic, for evidently a train was due, and he was anxious to close the bridge. He shouted to us to drop back with the tide; but anyone who has the slightest experience of the Broads knows a trick worth two of that. The dinghy is towed in these waters with only a foot of painter, and is thus right against the stern of the yacht, its stem-post covered with a good fender. Giving Robinson the helm, I was in the dinghy in a trice, and was pulling for all I was worth—*butting* the dinghy into the stern of the yacht, and *shoving* her through. The signalman no doubt breathed again, and the iron bridge clanged-to astern of us. We were clear.

"That was an inspiration." Robinson was impressed by my resource, and said that he "would never have thought of it." But I had, of course, to own up. It is quite an ordinary expedient on the Broads, useful when one just requires to tip the scale in a great hurry for a minute or two, and the water is likely to be too deep for the quant-pole. "Of course," I explained, "the yacht must have a flat transom, but most of them do here, like this one."

BROADLAND

The wind was less and less; and day was over. We decided to moor. A good stretch of hard bank offered—evidently a recognised place, and here we stayed. Sunset was in full tide, and it was molten gold.

Taking up one of the little rond-anchors, Robinson jeered at the smallness of it. "Puny little fellow," he said; and it *was* small enough in con-

ON THE WAVENEY

trast with the half-hundredweight mudhook on *Irene*. "But it's rather *genteel*, with its pretty white rope." Under my direction he took both rond-anchors ashore and worked them into the ground. Rond-anchors have the merit of answering their own purpose completely, and we were moored, fore and aft, alongside the bank.

Twilight was upon us—and moonrise too. The sunset as yet lingered, and the low moon opposite was broad and golden. The wind had gone to nothing, and that brimming water was unruffled; weed afloat upon it went by us, showing the movement of tide, but otherwise everything was still.

"This is sheer downright magic," said Robinson; "we'll never touch the like of it again."

Daylight was failing every moment, and now—out of the dusk to northward—came a strange vessel.

By winding reaches on and shining meres,
Between grey reed-ronds and green alder beds.

Black-sailed and silent, she grew into size, until—in the silence—we could hear the tap-tap of a man's feet on board her, and the slight ripple of her movement. With the long quant-pole against his shoulder, the stout fellow was pushing against the river-bottom, his feet tap-tapping the deck as he walked aft, pushing. A light showed from her cabin-window aft; and she slid by.

"A wherry?" Yes, it was the true type indigenous here, the one-sailed characteristic vessel of the Norfolk Broads. And Robinson said he had never seen a wherry before. "She looks strange, too, in this odd twilight," he added, "weird, unaccustomed, foreign. The whole thing is so unfamiliar; I can hardly believe I'm in England."

I raised the cabin-top, increasing the head-room,

and we went below to sort out our household affairs, and to prepare a meal. When we returned, sunset had faded; it was a moonlit night.

He was enthusiastic, and he did not stint his praise, but his voice was low. "One step ashore, and we go a-walking; how odd," he resumed; "it's another world from the salt water." The grass was dew-laden, and glittered under the moon.

In the stillness of night the whole country-side was ours. Lost suddenly in the heart of rural England, here we were—intimately at home in it because we need return to no village, with its lights and voices, for our lodging. Our little home was here; we were free of the whole silent moonlit landscape.

Our feet brushing the dew from the grass, we loitered slowly on in the moonlight. Now and again a fish jumped; there was no other sound. The water brimmed by us, still rising, with never a murmur. "Magical"; it was Robinson's word, and it was the only one.

Then we turned in. Robinson, half-drowsy, sat up in his bunk: "the riding-light," he said, "we haven't . . ."

"Don't want one here," I grunted, and he settled, reassured; if less sleepy, I might have told him that I made the same mistake myself on my own first visit to the Broads, waking with a guilty start in the same way. But he was already asleep, with the even breathing of a child.

Morning brought sunshine and wind; the wind having shifted was no longer fair for our passage, so

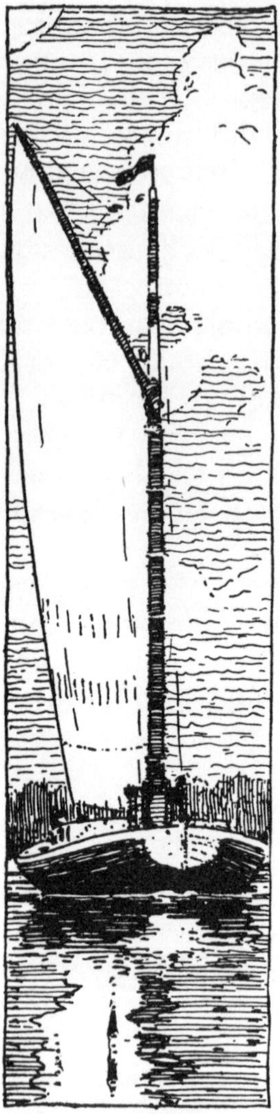

PLEASURE WHERRY

that we deferred our departure until turn of the tide. We explored the green banks by daylight; the little fleets and ditches were full of fish, the small trees rustled and bent with the wind, and the rooks were cawing. It was after midday when we rolled down a reef in the mainsail and got the rond-anchors on board.

"Can I? . . . thanks," Robinson said, as I offered him the helm. He took it with an expression preposterously grave, for he had in mind the clumsy fellows of yesterday. We pushed off.

His face cleared at once with a laugh of relief. "Why, she'll do everything but talk," he said; "she's a very knowing little packet."

That smile of sheer pleasure lingered on his face as he sailed her. His tacks were a trifle short at first; not all in a moment could he accustom himself to running his ship practically ashore before he put the helm down; he played for safety. But he soon began to gauge his distance; *whoop* came the wind, and laid the little yacht over, racing across the narrow river until—in very act of colliding with a rushy bank—he swerved her away and put her about, her stern actually brushing the tall green rush-stems as she came. Away, in a little scurry of foam, she shot straight for the twisted tree-roots opposite, and he foiled her always at the last instant, sending her straight into the wind's eye, with slatting canvas, until she filled for the next tack. And all the time she was eating up the distance to windward; and the wind was vigorous.

"More like the salt water to-day," he said. "There's less of the sleepy summer and the droning bees. Why, it's vigorous and noisy."

"Is it?"

I laughed at his expression of ludicrous surprise. At a curve of the river we had dropped into complete shelter of trees, and the wind was gone; we were dead still in hot sunshine.

But his attention was at once directed to something new, for he was pointing to an object which was a puzzle. What, by the same token, was it really? he was asking. Then it dawned upon him, for the thing began to change shape as its two sides were lowered; it was a drawbridge across the "Cut."

The Cut is an artificial waterway giving direct access to the Yare. And we followed it, the drawbridge being again raised in our favour, on payment of the toll, which is collected with a bag at the end of a long pole, held out to the yacht, Dutch fashion,

FROM BREYDON WATER (AT FOOT: ARMS OF YARMOUTH)

as she passes. We had entered the long, straight ditch beside the railway.

"Coming down in the world, eh?" said my companion; "first it's a toy river, and now, bothered if it isn't a canal. I suppose the next thing isn't a tunnel?"

We were really off the map of Suffolk now, and our little expedition to Norwich is outside the scope of this chapter. But we will follow on to Reedham, where Robinson gained his first touch of respect for these inland waters, when he asked to be allowed to try to pass the swing-bridge against the ebb. The ebb was pouring down the Yare, but we could stem it in the open, which induced him to petition for the effort. I told him he would fail, but I could see by his eye that he backed his own chances. The bridge happened to be open, and she sailed gamely right up to the entrance . . . paused, hovered and retreated. Facing the enemy, and dead straight on course, she came out of it stern-first, defeated. He said nothing, but steered her for the bank, where we tied up to await the turn of tide.

The wind died at sundown, when we were already under way and past Reedham with the brimming tide, and there was a faint mist that made everything vague in the moonrise. We seemed to swim through a world which was vaporous and unreal; moving with the whole liquid surface, we glided, and not one single sound disturbed the night.

Morning was less propitious when, after our return from Norwich, we were again at Reedham. A deluge of rain was the first sound; rioting over the cabin-top, we heard it as we awoke. But the drench of it was relenting as we made sail; and I took the helm to steer her through the bridge. I did not distinguish myself. Straight enough she went through, and then the wind on the other side caught her jib and turned her, despite my utmost effort to luff. I could not let my jib fly, because it was a "lazy-jib"; I sprang for'ard to the halliard, and brought the sail down by the run, but too late—for she was aground. It did not matter really; we were well clear of the bridge, and we quanted her off in a moment, but—well, never mind. "Bridge of ill omen," Robinson grinned, not in the least grieved, I was sure, to see the leader of the expedition put out of countenance in this way.

Down with the windings of the river we went, through a land of windmills, until the river opened into the wide stretch of Breydon Water, bringing us into sight of Suffolk again. Across the great lake we sailed (the channel through the tidal mud is marked by posts), and Yarmouth lay ahead. Reaching Yarmouth at slack water, we turned, and the young flood carried us back by the shore of Lothingland to the mouth of the Waveney.

BREYDON WATER

Breydon Water is a broad lake at high tide, but the inland sea of Roman times was probably twenty times as large. The present site of Yarmouth was then a sandbank, washed-over by the salt water. And the Yare, Waveney and Bure were arms of the sea, instead of insignificant little inland rivers. The whole face of things has changed.

It is said that one of the houses at Yarmouth, quite a long way from the present sea-shore, is built upon a Spanish galleon, wrecked there in the year of the Armada. Houses, in point of fact, had been built and rebuilt half a dozen times on that spot at Yarmouth in the fourteenth and fifteenth centuries, but the sea destroyed them. It was with

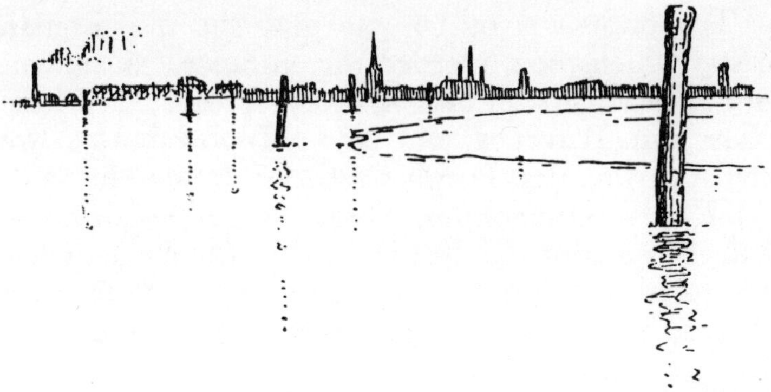

YARMOUTH, FROM BREYDON WATER (LOW TIDE)

the help of Dutch engineers that success was achieved in 1560. But Gorleston still eyes its neighbour askance, and the old rhyme is:

> "Gorleston was Gorleston ere Yarmouth begun,
> And will be Gorleston when Yarmouth is gone."

GORLESTON

To southward of us was now the old Roman castle which then guarded the entrance. Camden, in *Britannia* (first published in 1586), said: "Where Yare and Waveney join stood Cnobersburg; we call it at this day Burgh Castle." It was, he said, "the very Garianonum, where the Stablesian horse had their station." But in his time (he lived 1551–1625) it was "quite overgrown with briars and thorns, among which they now and then dig up Roman coins."

The Roman galleys were once here in the inlet; the stronghold was one of the forts of the "Saxon Shore," built to protect the coast against the incursions of the Saxon. It is all a matter of remote history, and the grey stone-work still stands.

One must not imagine the Roman vessels as small craft by contrast with ships of (say) 100 years ago. In actual fact it was not until the middle of the nineteenth century that Roman ships were materially surpassed in point of size.

Silent, and with many thoughts, we entered the Waveney. That grey custodian had somehow impressed us beyond the ordinary, and we were disinclined to chatter of it.

The grey morning had already been broken by shafts of sunlight, and the clouds were islanded in blue. Sunshine now flooded the landscape, unstinted. And, in this smiling Suffolk country-side, we relaxed; the tension was gone, the sense of awe had vanished. Somewhere beside the Fritton marshes we moored; for, though we had intended

ROMAN GALLEYS OFF GARIANONUM
(NOW KNOWN AS BURGH CASTLE)

to sail further, we liked this heathy land too well. So here we stayed.

After rambles ashore we were on board in twilight, and two wherries came by us, black-sailed, in the stillness. They were silhouetted, they and a single windmill, against the dim sky.

I wondered if the men had exchanged the ancient greeting. From old time, I have been told, the exchange has been this:

" How do you, sailor ? " says one skipper.

The other covers with a single glance the whole of his own trim vessel.

" There she goes," is his reply.

And these vessels are some of the most weatherly in the world. In a little yacht I have tried to match them in a hard breeze. I could sail their pace without difficulty, but as for keeping to weather in the way that they did, I found that it simply could not be done. It is as if the wherry had an instinct of her own. I recall one dusk when I was lying in the River Ant, and one of them slid by; the man was steering in that narrow cockpit, and there were lights from the little windows of the cabin.

"You're perfect marvels," I said, as the helmsman passed close beside me.

"' How so ? " said he, pleased.

" The way you keep to weather."

" Ah, it's the old wherry," he said, " *she* knows. She lives up at Irstead. She knows the way up to Irstead Street. She knows her way home."

Next day was riotous with wind, and we were

TO BECCLES, TO BECCLES,—TO BUY A BUNCH OF NETTLES;
HOME AGAIN, HOME AGAIN,—WHAT'S THE CLOCK, BUSSET?

away to Beccles, the old town which once grew rich on the herring fishery and later with the wool trade to the Continent. That nonsense verse, quoted below the picture, is of ancient but unknown origin, and its meaning is equally unknown. We moored just short of the town, the old church tower looking across the levels at us. Evening was again fine.

"We're trespassers here," Robinson asserted. "You can't talk of 'sea-borders' in mid-pastoral Suffolk."

"'Woody ways unbreathed on by the sea,'" I quoted. "Eh?"

"Exactly."

As if in answer, a small tug rounded the bend,

BROADS BOATS IN THE HARBOUR·

with a spritsail barge in tow. A wherry was just dropping down-stream, and the two of them passed. Wherries had hitherto been the lords of the water to us, large vessels and strong; but it was odd how the barge dwarfed the wherry. Yet each put the other in her place. The wherry was bred of the gentle streams, a fresh-water craft in every line of her; the barge was seasoned and salt of the sea. We read the name of her port; she came from Harwich.

"No locks between us and the sea," I commented. "It's all clear fairway, if rather roundabout. It all joins on."

. . . .

Back at Lowestoft in a day or two, we had really

completed our random adventure afloat. It was finished. And Robinson was happily spared one later occasion when I went on board *Irene* on a day in the autumn.

CHAPTER XIV

A FAREWELL

"PERSONALLY, I wouldn't," the boatbuilder had concluded, "I wouldn't go to sea in her myself." And his words had been like a blow struck unaware, that makes a man totter, dazed.

Intending to set sail at once, I had arrived at the hard, and the bags were already in the dinghy, to go on board. Then it was that the boatbuilder's hand upon my arm had drawn me back for a moment. "You'll use your own judgment, but I wouldn't go to sea in her *myself*." He had said it twice over.

The whole prospect (where cloud-shadow and sunshine chased over the landscape) was a picture, but the soul had suddenly gone from it for me. If the old yacht were staunch no longer, of what benefit then were all these?

I went on board.

Then, in the late evening, I was free to linger on deck and to look along the well-known waterway, seaward. Was it possible? *Could* it be that she, the hardy old yacht, the sturdy little sea-gull of the strenuous seaways—*could* it be that she was really finished? That never again this tiller (and I handled it, fast though it were in its tiller-lines) would steer her through the bicker of tide or the steep grey seas outside? That those halliards would never set the mainsail again? It seemed incredible. No, "there's life in the old ship yet," I repeated; and yet . . . and yet . . . The doubt was there.

"Them old yachts," an old boatbuilder had said to me once, "them old yachts, you're always puttin' your hand in your pocket; always somethin'." One may hold no brief for his general proposition, but his words came back to me that evening. Yes, I could recall more of what he had said. "Them old yachts; put 'em up on the slipway, and then the blokes begin. It's a timber here, it's this an' it's that, it's this an' that. An' there you are, afore her ballast's shipped again an' she's afloat, what sort o' bill have they run you up? Get off with fifty quid, perhaps, more like a hundred. An' what have you got for it all, all said an' done? What have you got? *An old boat.*"

In the twilight, some distant birds—far away over the creeks—sent their lonely cries; there was no other sound. Yachts at their moorings glimmered in the half-light. They were able boats no doubt, fit enough and ready to go to sea. And this poor old gallant companion of mine, she was the only cripple. It was a poignant moment.

For she assumed individuality so much in retrospect. The hand upon the helm was forgotten; the old yacht herself it was that had done these things, as if unaided. She it was that, slipping out of some creek in the dawn, had been furtive and secret; for so she was wont to glide, as if fearful of disturbing the shadows. Or, if the morning were boisterous, she was ready. As she filled away on the reefed mainsail—her moment had come, and she heeled joyously, ramping full. She was at sea. The spray was driving, the waves pounded in streaming green water upon the deck of her, but she only shook herself free of it all and lifted again; the strong wind hollowed her canvas into full curves, and she drove solidly, a thing trenchant, purposeful, alive. In a hundred places I could think of her thus, companion and almost guide. And now?

The chorus of a deep-sea chanty, inappropriate enough in its general bearing, ran in my head unchanging, with that everlasting reiteration of a tag of tune. Over and over the same words drummed that evening, as I lounged in the twilight with heavy heart:

> "Oh, don't you hear our old man say,
> *Good-bye, fare you well; good-bye, fare you well.*"

The refrain was not really what the old man said in the very least; but the words sorted themselves out in that fashion, and the two lines ran on unending. "Good-bye, fare you well"; it was a kind of far-off wail from the sea. "Good-bye, fare you well"; the same words again.

I went below to supper under the little cabin lamp. Bright and homely as ever, the narrow region was full of its own associations. It, too, must yield its memories. One could hear the whine of the wind, and the rattle of water on deck at some exposed anchorage; there, ticking busily beside the barometer, was the old alarm-clock which had hounded me forth so often into dark dawns or to moonlight night. Here were the bunks which (hard enough, heaven knows!) had been a couch of luxury ecstatic when—after twenty-four hours on deck—one has pulled off the dripping oilskins.

As I sat in the orderly cabin to-night, I could see in fancy quite a different setting. No table-cloth, for certain, and no effort towards order. An overflow of plates, tins and bottles would have found its way to the floor, where some stray pilot book or chart would still be lying. Steam and smells of cookery from the fo'c's'le would possess the cabin, the port-holes of which would be misted and streaming by reason of the dead cold of the night outside. And we two, my shipmate and I, would be squatted there, positively dropping forwards, so dead sleepy after a long passage that now (at 2 a.m. perhaps) we were barely able to summon resolution to clear the crockery outside and settle the bunks. We were tumbling into sleep as we sat, until some huge effort broke the spell, and we clattered and blundered for a few resolute seconds before the light was dowsed, and authentic slumber had claimed us. Yes, it had been a good life.

I went out on deck again, and the sunset had almost faded, but there was a slip of moon. The creek had a sense of isolation which possessed its own charm. The tide was low; it had uncovered the tidal flats.

I am wont thus to linger on deck; it has ever been a habit. One silently absorbs the sensation of everything; the soul of the place is not withheld.

The tangled water-world of these creeks has its own shadowy past, vague as the autumn mists upon it. Time out of mind, some ragged populace picked a livelihood, niggard enough, about its borders. And to those old dwellers it was often unfriendly. Ague-haunted fens, some of these sea-borders had an ill name, and sportsmen of Defoe's day, who came wild-fowling here, were apt to return with an "ague on their backs, which they find a heavier load than the fowls they have shot."

But we of these later generations, coming in our staunch little yachts, seem to have been accepted by the local deities without suspicion or rebuff. In our little cabins we sleep through nights when the dank mist is heavy upon marsh and salting, and a water-logged world stretches long fingers of ooze landward for miles about us.

And late arrivals we are. This old yacht, she is an old boat, and she began life as a Paglesham smack, being converted I know not when. In days of her youth she must have wandered about the shores and inlets when cruising yachts were few, and anchorages were possessed by smacks only.

"*Old*, is she? Well, I shouldn't wonder;" and the old boatbuilder had smiled reflectively as he said it.

I had tried now and again to get some authentic details of her history, but without success, and could only estimate her age by guess-work.

"How old do you suppose?" I asked him.

"Well," and he lingered over the monosyllable; "well, I s'pose she's old as I am; and that won't see sixty any more," he confided.

She lived her old life as a fishing-boat, a smack that followed generations of smacks. On the deck of this old boat, as upon the decks of her own predecessors through the centuries, the full trawl has been dumped with a thud. Perhaps the dark estuary has glimmered sombrely about her in a moonless night. As the trawl thudded on deck, there would be a scatter of pattering sound everywhere, as the crabs innumerable released themselves and scurried to every corner, seeking escape. As now, the heavy boots of fishermen have *crunched* down on crabs unnumbered, and the men have shovelled them back, in broken heaps, resentful of their useless existence. Then the pocket of the trawl would yield its catch. A-glimmer in the dark, the white undersides of dab, sole and plaice are seen; and, sorted from all the cumber of seaweed and stones and rubbish, they are hoarded apart. Then, cleared again and empty, the trawl once more splashes in the dark water and the work is renewed.

. . . . . .

She has been a dainty little lady, despite her smack ancestry. And a wonderful companion as, after periods of inaction at the mooring, she used to tremble into life, away once more on the wind. And so amenable and mannerly she was: "Wunnerful handy, yes, I see she is," an old boatman said; "yes, a child could handle her."

She was the work of shipwrights who had learned

their craft through generations in Essex and Suffolk, counties which once were able to build first-rates for the Crown. Think of the lustihood of all those generations, stout Normans and vigorous Elizabethans, who have worked and joked and sung in shipyards long forgotten. Silence and shadow have taken them. They are gone. But their traditions have been passed down, and their old ship-sense—adapted to their own simpler needs as fishermen—has evolved the beautiful local smacks. Mersea smacks on the south coast were mistaken for yachts, such a turn of speed was theirs, so fine and graceful their lines; and yet they were built for mere workaday purposes.

The fine sense of those centuries of shipwrights was in the building of this old boat. Her decks, sixty years ago, were trodden by fishermen, then jovial youngsters—young husbands, perhaps, with girls ashore as youthful wives. The men have had their day; they are all dead now. And at long last the old boat is to follow.

She is only a detail; just an unconsidered leaf in the autumn. The myriad other ships of these waters have had their personalities, their own whims and habits, as—alive in sunlight—they have sailed the Essex or Suffolk seas. And they, too, are gone.

It is only one more ship. She must go. I must leave her. Those old deep-sea chanties, words also echoing from the lips of men now long dead, they have a quality of refrain which has kept them alive for generations at sea; they run of themselves, and the words came unbidden:

"The work was hard, the voyage was long,
Leave her, Johnny, leave her.
The seas were high, the gales were strong,
And it's time for us to leave her."

. . . .

That was the mood of the silent nightfall—farewell. And sober thought by daylight and in winter-time ashore did not vary its effect. The position grew clearer. Had the internal accommodation of the old boat been good and sufficient, she was still worth a new lease of life. If, alternatively, I were a practical man with time on my hands, and could do the work myself, I need not hesitate. But, as it was, she must go.

Her gear unshipped, she lay forlornly, a thing dilapidated. People came and looked at her; they remarked her scanty head-room, and shook their heads. The condition of her hull was no secret, the need for outlay was frankly stated; and gradually the little flow of callers waned, and she lay alone in her mud berth, forlorn, abandoned.

On my new yacht—resplendent in her white paint—I sailed into that very creek, within sight and hail of the old ship. I could fancy that she was aware. I felt a rebuke almost—in her silence and resignation. I landed and stood on the foreshore beside her; and, if she were mutely unhappy, so also at that moment was I.

Finally, someone was minded to have her as a house-boat, to remove her deck and build a superstructure. But she was not to degenerate thus. The eyes of local smacksmen had been upon her.

Not yet to die and rot forgotten, she became the centre of a knot of industrious fellows, while ballast was unshipped, the hull explored, old paint-work burnt off, and liberal tar administered, so that—Heaven helping—she will for years yet have the feet of fishermen upon her decks, and the trawls will again bring the fish on board of her. In the fullness of her age she becomes a smack once more.

THE END

INDEX